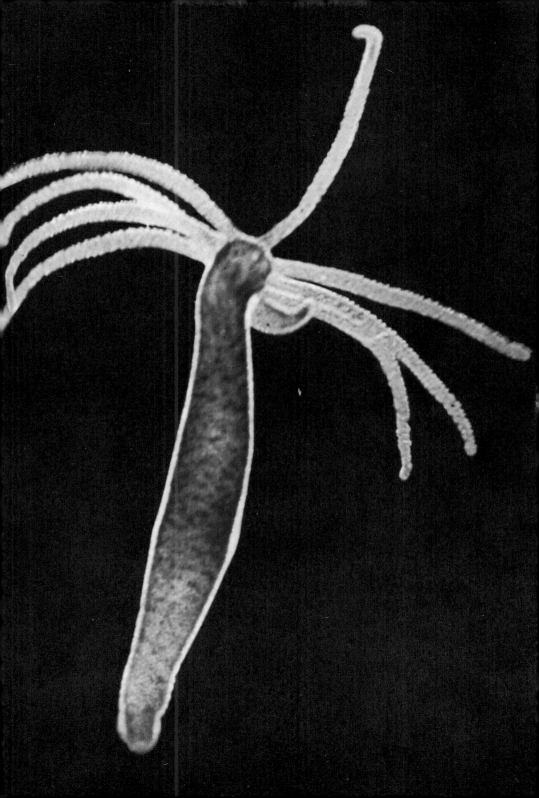

A Chanticleer Press Edition

INVERTEBRATES
OF NORTH
AMERICA

LORUS AND MARGERY MILNE

Doubleday & Company, Inc., New York

ANIMAL LIFE OF NORTH AMERICA SERIES

Birds of North America
by Austin L. Rand

Fishes of North America
by Earl S. Herald

Insects of North America
by Alexander and Elsie Klots

Mammals of North America
by Robert T. Orr

Reptiles and Amphibians of North America
by Alan Leviton

For Ralph and Mildred Buchsbaum

Half-title page photograph: Freshwater Hydra

Title page photograph: Feather Star

All rights reserved under International and
Pan-American Copyright Conventions

Published in the United States by Doubleday &
Company, Inc., New York. Distributed in Canada
by Doubleday Canada Limited, Toronto

Planned and produced by Chanticleer Press, Inc., New York

Manufactured by Amilcare Pizzi, S.p.A., Milan, Italy

Library of Congress Catalog Card Number 76-147-355

Contents

Introduction

Acquaintance with nonhuman members of the Animal Kingdom generally begins with the warm-blooded mammals and birds. Fishes seem distinct enough, although they come in almost twice as many different forms as all of the world's mammals and birds together. Reptiles and amphibians are equally cold-blooded possessors of a backbone—a jointed vertebral column that provides support for the body. Yet these animals, whose structure is most like our own, account for only about 1/28 of the number of animals on earth. We commonly group all of the others as animals without backbones, or invertebrates.

The invertebrates are either cold-blooded or have no blood at all. Although many of them have a head and a right side and a left, almost none possesses just two pairs of appendages—arms, legs, wings, or fins. The invertebrates with three pairs of legs are mostly insects; they constitute fully 20/28 of the total variety of animal life. The other invertebrates, with either more legs or none at all, account for about 7/28, or a quarter, of the different kinds of animals and provide the subject for this book.

These invertebrates, exclusive of insects, include the vast majority of marine animals, as well as many that live in fresh waters, in soil, or on land in forests, grasslands, deserts, and the tundras both of polar regions and mountain slopes. Those whose habitat is the sea are known from fossils to have had ancestors in the salty aquatic realm for more than 600 million years. Among them are worms, crustaceans, mollusks, echinoderms, and lowly sponges, whose ancestry can be traced 100 million years before the earliest known vertebrate. The first colonists from the seas into fresh waters came later, about 400 million years ago. This was the route that led, however, through swamplands into moist soil and onto land. The fossil record shows that spiders have been pursuing insects and other small terrestrial animals for less than 350 million years; in earlier geological periods no land life of any kind is known. Similarly the grasslands and tundras seem to have supported the highly specialized invertebrates that live there now for less than 70 million years.

In North America, virtually no animals of any kind have ancestors which were in the same locality for 25,000 years because the climate changed so radically following the Ice Age. The opportunities on land have undergone major alterations as the glaciers melted and the vegetation spread from southern states to higher latitudes and altitudes. Living things in the oceans gained some

ARCTIC
(circumpolar)

Greenland

Boreal

Boreal

Boreal

LEUTIAN
ubprovince)

EGONIAN

ACADIAN
(subprovince)

VIRGINIAN
(subprovince)

CAROLINIAN

ALIFORNIAN

Subtropical

CARIBBEAN

PANAMANIAN

Tundra

Taiga

Mixed forests

Grasslands

Deciduous forests

Broad leaf evergreens and deciduous conifers

Biogeographic Provinces of North America

7

protection from severe cold. The location of the coastline changed markedly as the glaciers turned to water and ran into the seas. The whole continent underwent readjustment from being warped by the weight of overlying ice. Along the Atlantic coast in particular, a plain, on which primitive American Indians may have hunted huge mammoths, sank below the waves during the last 15,000 years. In places this plain was 200 miles broad. Now it is the sea floor along the continental shelf and a hunting ground for hungry codfishes and other marine creatures that search out invertebrates such as sea worms and crabs.

Today, the coastal invertebrates that a beachcomber can encounter show a geographic distribution that reflects both the historic past and modern living conditions. The temperature of the water in winter and summer provides some limitations. More significant is the availability of food, especially of the small green plants that drift along the coast and the organic matter that is flushed from tidal gutters through the saltmarshes. All of these factors combine to maintain differences between the marine invertebrates along the American west coast in a "Californian" province south of Monterey, and in an "Oregonian" province northward almost to Alaska. A transition zone, called the Aleutian subprovince, borders southwestern Alaska, while the cold waters of the "Boreal" province along the west coast hold an invertebrate fauna much like that around Hudson Bay, the Atlantic shores of Labrador, southern Greenland and Iceland, and northern Newfoundland. A matching transition zone (the Acadian subprovince) extends along the New England coast to Cape Cod, where it is largely kept distinct from the Virginian extension (north of Cape Hatteras) of the "Carolinian" province. The Carolinian is found on both sides of Florida and around the Gulf of Mexico almost to the Rio Grande. There it meets a tropical Caribbean component that is represented also at the tip of Florida, in the Bahamas and to the northward limit of reef-forming corals in Bermuda.

On land, the invertebrates tend to match the environmental conditions that determine the possible location of tundras at high latitudes and high altitudes, of coniferous forests rich in spruce and fir (the taiga) from Alaska to northern New England and just lower than the alpine tundras, of the deciduous forest in the middle Atlantic states, of the evergreen forest of pines and broad-leaved trees such as magnolias in the southeastern states, of the great grasslands in the Central Plains, of the deserts and scrublands in the Southwest, and of the evergreen forests of the Pacific slopes from the redwood empire in California and Oregon to southern Alaska with its tall Douglas-fir and Sitka spruce.

Some invertebrates, such as the sea urchins and other echinoderms, occur only in marine habitats, but are found all around the coastline of North America. Others, such as the sponges and jellyfishes, are strictly aquatic and mostly marine, but have a few representatives in fresh waters. The lobsters of the North Atlantic coast are not too different from the crayfishes of rivers and lakes, although neither type of animal can tolerate for more than a few minutes the natural environment of the other. Of the invertebrates, other than insects whose ancestors invaded the land long ago, many have become adapted for life under so many different conditions that the same animal can be met on sea beaches, and high mountains, in deserts, tundras, grasslands, forests, caves, soil, and perhaps fresh waters.

The versatility and limitations shown by invertebrate animals are consequences of structural features and their function. These features evolved over an immensity of time and include many that are so constant that scientists can use them confidently as the basis for classification. The broader details, especially those that become evident as an individual animal develops through embryonic stages, seem especially fundamental. The finer details may be more recent in origin and serve to allow each species to follow a unique way of life. To survive in a world with limited resources, it must compete as little as possible for space and food with its neighbors of other kinds. Just as the number of individuals of a species that can find a place for themselves is a measure of the success of the species, so too the number of distinct species in a subdivision of the Animal Kingdom often indicates the prosperity of the subdivision.

In dividing the animal world into categories, scientists look for clusters of similarities rather than distinctive single features. Each feature, such as whether the body is segmented, is likely to be subject to considerable variation and some outright exceptions to any rule. Some clusters seem more impressive than others, and value judgments are necessary in deciding which to regard as the primary categories, called phyla. General agreement has been found for recognizing 22 phyla, which containing the following approximate number of species:

Phylum Protozoa: 28,350
Phylum Porifera: 4,800
Phylum Cnidaria: 5,300
Phylum Ctenophora: 80
Phylum Platyhelminthes: 12,700
Phylum Nemertea: 800

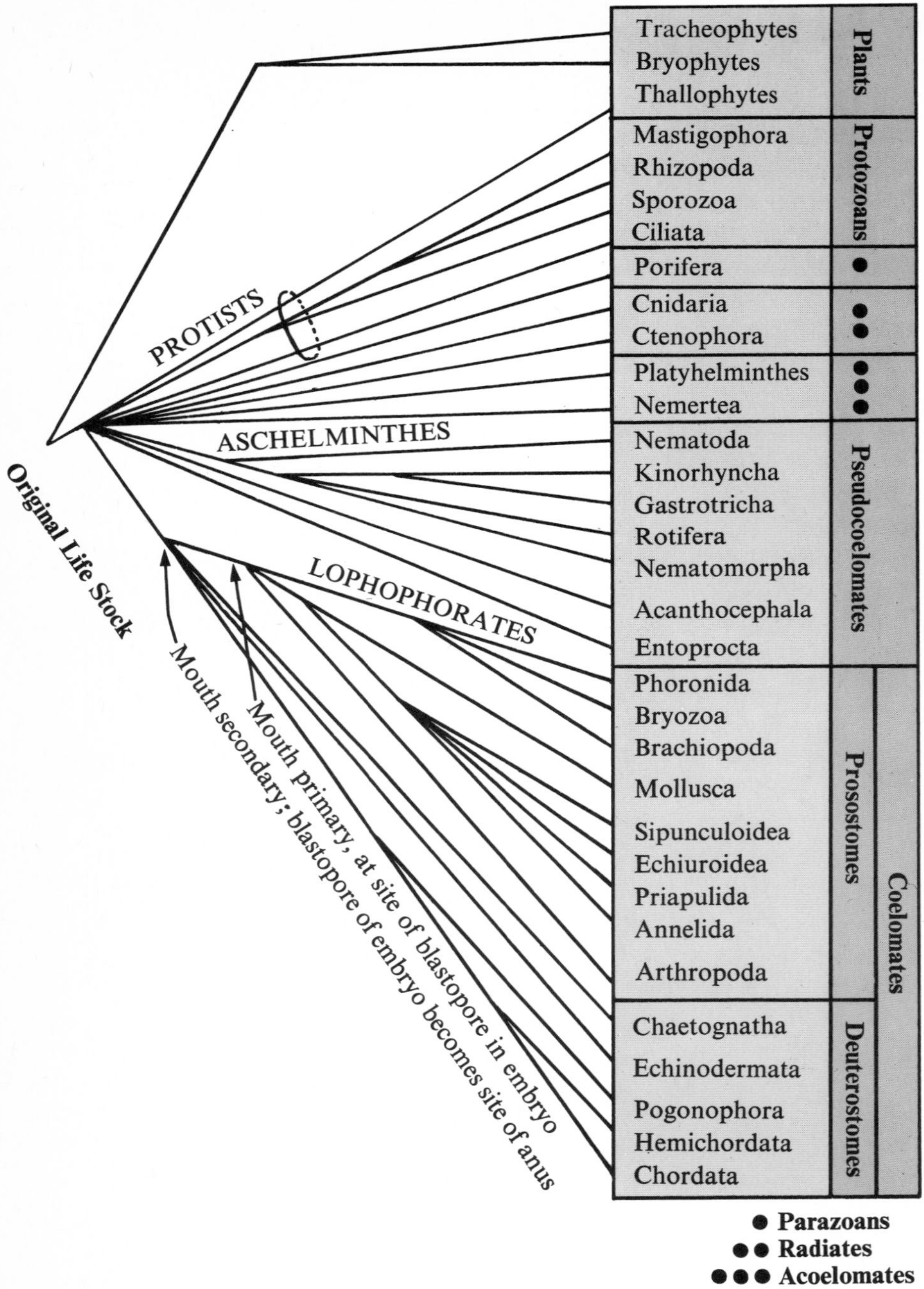

	Plants
Tracheophytes Bryophytes Thallophytes	Plants
Mastigophora Rhizopoda Sporozoa Ciliata	Protozoans
Porifera	●
Cnidaria Ctenophora	●●
Platyhelminthes Nemertea	●●●
Nematoda Kinorhyncha Gastrotricha Rotifera Nematomorpha Acanthocephala Entoprocta	Pseudocoelomates
Phoronida Bryozoa Brachiopoda Mollusca Sipunculoidea Echiuroidea Priapulida Annelida Arthropoda	Prosostomes
Chaetognatha Echinodermata Pogonophora Hemichordata Chordata	Deuterostomes

PROTISTS

ASCHELMINTHES

LOPHOPHORATES

Original Life Stock

Mouth primary, at site of blastopore in embryo

Mouth secondary; blastopore of embryo becomes site of anus

Coelomates

● Parazoans
●● Radiates
●●● Acoelomates

Invertebrate Family Tree

Phylum Aschelminthes: 12,800
Phylum Acanthocephala: 500
Phylum Entoprocta: 75
Phylum Phoronida: 18
Phylum Bryozoa: 3,500
Phylum Brachiopoda: 230
Phylum Mollusca: 45,000
Phylum Sipunculoidea: 250
Phylum Echiuroidea: 150
Phylum Priapulida: 8
Phylum Annelida: 8,500
Phylum Arthropoda (not including insects): 90,000
Phylum Chaetognatha: 50
Phylum Echinodermata: 6,000
Phylum Pogonophora: 100
Phylum Hemichordata: 80
Phylum Chordata (not including vertebrates): 1,325.

Scientists unanimously agree that the microscopic, single-celled forms, such as amebas, euglenas, slipper animalcules, and malaria parasites, have more in common with one another than with the many-celled, macroscopic animals and plants with which everyone is familiar. Yet should euglenas, which have chlorophyll and can make their own food from inorganic nutrients and water if they have sunlight, be regarded as animals or plants? Traditionally, the botanists have made a place for euglenas in the Plant Kingdom, grouping them with other chlorophyll-bearing single cells of similar type in the Phylum Euglenophyta. This judgment, however, rejects all single cells that lack chlorophyll and rely upon organic foods, no matter how similar these forms of life are in other features. The zoologists insist that the possession or lack of chlorophyll, and hence the mode of nutrition, is less important than the other similarities among these single cells. This leads to classifying the euglenas, and similar nongreen cells, in Phylum Protozoa of the Animal Kingdom.

In recent years, an impressive number of biologists have relegated all of these single-celled types of life to a third kingdom: the Protista, or protists. This decision merely shifts the dilemma to a different area. Should the third kingdom include also all of the plants that botanists have long regarded as comprising the Subkingdom Thallophyta in the Plant Kingdom: the multicellular algae, the multicellular fungi, the single-celled bacteria, and perhaps the lichens?

A Variety of North American Invertebrates: Top left, Ringed Top Shell and Star Fish; top right, Snail; bottom left, Heteropod; bottom center, Yellow Jelly Fish; bottom right, Orb Weaver

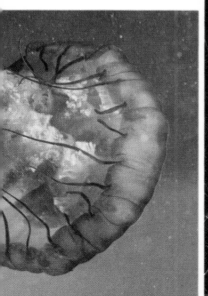

Expressed another way, is an ameba more like a giant kelp and a puffball than it is like the individual cells that comprise a sponge? At the unicellular level, the border between the Animal Kingdom and the Plant Kingdom seems vague. In this book, we retain euglenas and their kin as members of Phylum Protozoa and as invertebrate animals. Their differences from other invertebrates can be recognized by assigning them to a separate subkingdom.

The sequence of the phyla in the preceding list and the succeeding chapters follows a progression, but should not be regarded as a "ladder of life." So far as is known, all animals have an ancestry of approximately equal length. Modern protozoans are evolving new adaptations that make them more successful as protozoans—not features that transform them into sponges (Porifera). Sponges are not turning into cnidarians, nor echinoderms into chordates. The progression, instead, begins with single cells that can perform all life functions without associating into cooperating groups. Next are the sponges, in which cooperating cells show incredible versatility without losing their need for community action. A further step, among the cnidarians, is the organization of the multicellular body into two distinct layers of cells, an outer and an inner, with different roles. All other animals possess at least a third and intermediate layer of cells with specific functions as part of a greater division of labor. The cnidarians, comb-jellies (Ctenophora) and flatworms (Platyhelminthes) have no more than a blind digestive cavity, and use the mouth for both feeding and discharge of undigested wastes. Yet this similarity may be less significant than the fact that coelenterates and comb-jellies have an underlying radial symmetry, whereas the flatworms are bilaterally symmetrical. So are the parasitic thorny-headed worms (Acanthocephala) and the strange beard worms (Pogonophora), which lack a digestive tract altogether.

The members of all other phyla seem more efficient in having a tubular gut from mouth to anus; they also start out life as bilaterally symmetrical embryos. Yet the simplest animals with a tubular gut, the ribbon worms (Nemertea) are much like flatworms, particularly in having all of the volume around the inner organs filled with cells (a mesenchyme). Scientists group the ribbon worms and flatworms together as lacking a body cavity of any kind, and hence "acoelomates."

The roundworms and the members of several other groups placed with them in the Phylum Aschelminthes resemble the spiny-headed worms (Acanthocephala) and the entoprocts (Entoprocta) in having a body cavity. But the embryonic development that provides this space for fluids inside the cylindrical body does not produce any lining layer of cells. For this reason the body cavity is referred to as a pseudocoele and the members of these phyla as "pseudo-coelomates." None of them has any musculature around the gut except at the anterior and posterior end. Food is stuffed into the tube in front and must find its own way to the other end, where muscles do help in defecation.

By contrast, the members of phyla from Chaetognatha to Chordata inclusive (but again omitting the beard worms) have a muscular sheath around the gut. In beard worms embryonic development provides a body cavity lined by a recognizable tissue, called the peritoneum. This feature makes the cavity a coelom, and these phyla the "coelomates." In mollusks and arthropods the coelom remains small and some of its roles seem taken over by expansions (blood sinuses) of the circulatory system.

Viewed as a three-dimensional tree to show what is known of ancestral origins, the protozoan line is seen as branching from ground level and the sponges only a small distance higher on the main trunk that represents the animals. The next branch up divides as soon as it leaves the trunk, one division leading to the cnidarians and ctenophores and the other to the flatworms and nemerteans. A further branch represents the pseudocoelomates, dividing off the thorny-headed worms and entoprocts before splitting into the distinctive classes of the aschelminths. The remainder of the trunk is coelomate, with two main branches. One leads to the segmented worms (Annelida), the arthropods, the mollusks, and several lesser phyla—hence to the majority of invertebrates and to most kinds of animal life. The other branch gives rise only to the chordates, the acorn worms (Hemichordata), the beard worms and the echino-derms. The invertebrate representatives of this branch are exclusively marine and are so unlike the familiar vertebrate animals that it is hard to credit them with being kin of ours.

The Protozoans *(Phylum Protozoa)*

Protozoans, literally the "first animals," have made their mark, despite their small size, since the very beginning of the fossil record. Live protozoans were discovered in 1674 by a Dutch cloth merchant whose hobby was the construc-tion of simple microscopes with lenses of his own making. He found the "animalcules" swimming in a drop of water collected from a small inland lake

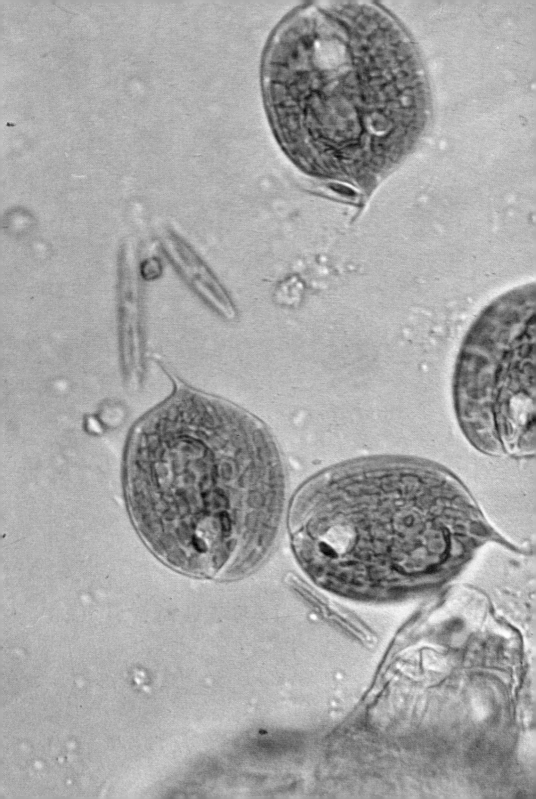

near his home in Delft. Soon he located others in many other samples of standing water that contained decaying organic matter. Since these same kinds of protozoans live in similar places in North America and most other parts of the world, it is easy to repeat his observations and to improve upon them, using the far better compound microscopes that are available today.

A few kinds of protozoans are large enough to notice with the unaided eye. Mostly they are free-living denizens of swamp water and bird baths, and nourish themselves on smaller protozoans and bacteria. Far more members of this phylum are as small as the malaria parasite, which is about 1/25,000 inch in diameter and able to grow, then reproduce, inside a single red blood cell.

Size is not the major criterion for membership in this fascinating phylum, for some protozoans are larger than the smallest insects. Instead, the distinction lies in the ability of a single cell to carry on all of life's processes within its boundaries, usually as an independent individual.

Microscopic dimensions give a protozoan real advantages. Its surface area is huge in comparison with the bulk of living organism that must be nourished. This makes the exchange of oxygen and carbon dioxide through the boundary membrane simple and, for those cells that live on organic material, the absorption of food equally easy. Moreover, the small body needs only a little nourishment—comparatively few molecules of food—before it doubles its dimensions and is ready to divide. One cell becoming two and the two growing quickly to repeat the process is a common program in reproduction.

Although some protozoans move about quite actively and respond to the direction of light or the concentration of dissolved materials in ways that may bring them to food, they cannot travel fast. They propel themselves in various ways but take minutes to move an inch. Only in water can they direct their activities. They are helpless on land or in air and must survive desiccation if they are to be carried by a breeze, like particles of dust, from one wet place to another.

The classes of protozoans are distinguished according to the means, if any, whereby the cells move from place to place.

The Flagellates (Class Mastigophora)

These protozoans possess one or more whiplike flagella, which they extend into the surrounding water either to pull themselves along or to spin themselves on a longitudinal axis. Flagellates that have more than one flagellum may produce both types of motion simultaneously and travel in a fairly straight line. In reproduction, the full-grown cell ordinarily duplicates the flagella at its anterior end and then divides lengthwise into two half-sized cells, which grow to repeat the process.

Among the most common and widespread of the green euglenas is *Euglena gracilis*, no more than 1/500 inch long, which thrives in ponds and puddles and can tolerate brackish water to a salinity two-fifths that of the open sea. More spectacular is *E. rubrum*, which is slightly larger and contains hundreds of minute red granules as well as dozens of green chlorophyll-containing structures inside each cell. During the middle of the day, it disperses the red granules throughout the body and conceals its chlorophyll. From late afternoon until the next morning, *E. rubrum* concentrates its red particles in one central region and lets the green show. In a barnyard pond, where this species responds to nutrients from animal wastes and becomes unbelievably abundant, it colors the water—particularly the surface scum—dark red through most of the day and changes to bright green as the light fades. Reproductive individuals commonly develop a thick waterproof wall to become a "cyst." In this encysted condition they tolerate drought and a wide range of temperatures from below freezing to above 150° F. Cysts can ride from pond to pond on the muddy feet of birds or be blown as particles in dust from one dried-up pond to another that contains water.

Along with *E. rubrum*, or in place of it in waters that are contaminated with manure, a more plantlike flagellate *(Chlamydomonas)* often becomes so abundant that it makes the water opaque green. *Chlamydomonas* has an almost spherical body, a single cup-shaped structure containing its chlorophyll, and two flagella of almost equal length. It has a rigid cellulose cell wall and stores energy in the form of starch, whereas euglenas are flexible and store a different carbohydrate (paramylum). Very similar in appearance to *Chlamydomonas* is *Haematococcus*, which is like *Euglena rubrum* in being able to mask its chlorophyll with red granules. *Haematococcus* reproduces near the surface of snow fields in the Rocky Mountains and the Alps, often coloring the melting snow a bright pink. "Pink snow" has its counterpart in "red rain," when *Haematococcus* proliferates in rain barrels and puddles after a storm in warm weather.

In ponds and near the shores of shallow lakes, plantlike flagellates form colonies that challenge the scientist to explain cellular interactions and that delight the microscopist because of the handsome symmetries. In colonies of *Gonium*, the virtually identical cells associate in some species to form simple flat

Dinoflagellates

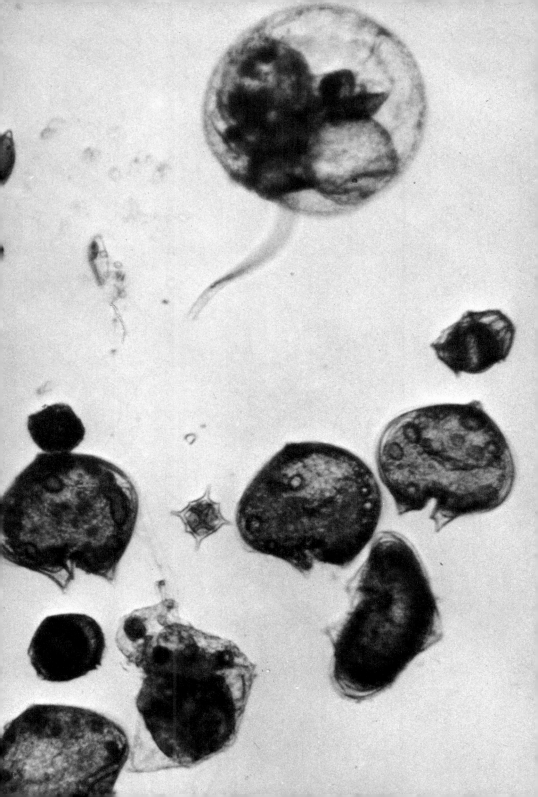

discs composed of no more than four cells; in other species a central foursome is surrounded by a dozen others and embedded in a common gelatinous matrix. In *Volvox*, the hundreds to thousands of associated cells form the surface of a hollow sphere which rolls along, propelled by the coordinated activity of the many cells, each of which bears two flagella.

Near the sea surface and along coasts, the most abundant flagellates are those known as dinoflagellates (from the Greek *dinos* which signifies both whirling and terrible). A dinoflagellate has an encircling groove, the "girdle," from which the flagellum protrudes, that keeps it spinning, and a lengthwise groove, the "sulcus," out of which projects a second flagellum that may pull the cell along or capture for it particles of food such as bacteria. *Noctiluca scintillans* is one of the largest, reaching 1/20 inch in diameter, and most conspicuous at night off oceanic shores all over the world. Stimulated by wave action or by a moving ship or even a nocturnal swimmer—person or porpoise or fish—a *Noctiluca* produces a brief bright flash of light, like a luminous protest at being disturbed. Suddenly the wave or the water scintillates with these minute sources of bioluminescence, then goes dark again. By day, in protected bays where these faintly pinkish cells have become especially abundant, they may produce large areas where the surface water has the appearance of pale tomato soup.

Most dinoflagellates produce a heavy shell of cellulose, often marked off into distinct plates and always grooved to let the flagella operate. From pores in the shell they may extend a fine network of cytoplasm as a trap for bacteria and other prey. *Peridinium* species, whose shells resemble twin igloos fitted together base to base with the girdle groove between, and *Ceratium*, which has three long hornlike projections from its shell, are often abundant in surface waters of lakes and the sea. These abundant protozoans serve important roles in converting very small particles of organic matter into bodies large enough to be caught by anchovies, herrings and other fishes that strain out the coarser plankton.

Under climatic conditions that are not fully understood, the dinoflagellates *Gymnodinium* and *Gonyaulax* reproduce prolifically along sea coasts until each quart of water contains five million or so of these armored cells. They color the water, causing "red tides," and at the same time both compete for oxygen and free toxic materials, causing the death of so many fishes that the beach is soon littered with rotting bodies. Barnacles, shrimps, crabs, oysters, clams and other coastal animals die. Fishermen and shellfishermen cease operations, sometimes for several years, until conditions change and colonists restock the coast with living things.

Freshwater Ameba (Amoeba)

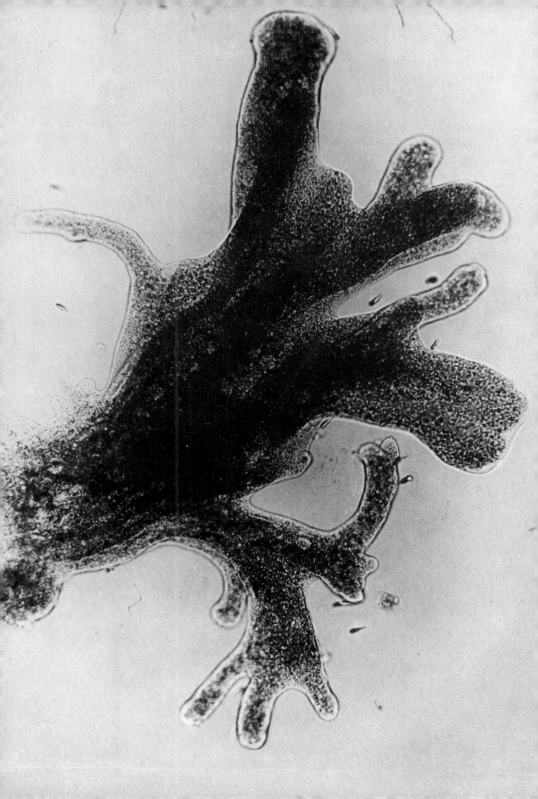

In America north of Mexico, only a returning traveler from tropical countries is likely to be troubled by an infection with flagellates that cause major diseases. From Mexico to northern Argentina, one hazard is *Trypanosoma cruzi* which causes the debilitating anemia and nervous symptoms known as Chagas' disease; this parasite is transferred to man from wild animals by a triatomid bug that enters houses and takes blood meals from sleeping people. In Africa south of the great deserts, the closely related trypanosomes of several species cause a deadly sleeping sickness in man and equally destructive nagana disease in cattle. The tsetse flies of genus *Glossina* carry the infection to man and livestock from many different kinds of native animals, which are immune to these parasites.

In North America, a person is far more likely to become infected with a *Trichomonas* or a *Giardia*. *T. tenax*, which may be transferred in a kiss and lives in the human mouth, perhaps contributing to the destructive action of organisms producing pyorrhea. *T. vaginalis* is found in the vagina of more than one woman in five and sometimes in the male urinary tract and prostate gland. Whether it causes damage or merely feeds on bacteria that are also present has not been clearly established. *Giardia* causes a diarrhea.

Flagellates with more than a dozen flagella live in the intestines of wood roaches and most termites. Some, but not all, of them have the ability to digest the cellulose in wood fibers eaten by the roach or termite and are essential to the nourishment of the insect.

The Amebas and Their Kin (Class Sarcodina)

Through most of their lives, the members of this class move and capture food by putting forth lobelike projections of their own cytoplasm. The whole cell may flow into this extension of itself, called a pseudopodium or "false foot," or it may simply use the projection as a sticky surface to which bacteria and other particles will adhere. Amebas are lacking in a definite form, but many of their relatives take on more distinctive shapes by enclosing or supporting themselves by means of skeletons of some kind.

The widespread *Amoeba proteus* of freshwater ponds can often be found flowing through itself on the under side of a lily pad. There the ameba finds short lengths of filamentous algae, smaller protozoans, clusters of bacteria, and other suitable foods. It manages to extend a cup-shaped pseudopodium around these particles and close the escape route. This places a droplet of water, called

Marine Foraminiferan (Discorbis)

a "food vacuole," inside the cell. The ameba secretes digestive enzymes into the food vacuole and later absorbs the organic products of digestion. Undigested residues remain inside and are eventually discarded as the cell lets the vacuole lag until it opens through the cell surface and vanishes. An ameba that is well nourished has many granules of glycogen as a food reserve and grows until it reaches a critical volume. Then the processes of cell division begin. Soon the cell separates into two of equal size.

Averaging 1/50 inch long when about to divide, *A. proteus* is a large member of its genus. Smaller ones live in ponds and wet soil. A much bigger kind, *Chaos chaos*, attains a length of 1/4 inch in marshes from New Jersey to South Carolina. Unlike the smaller amebas, which have a single nucleus, *Chaos* has dozens of nuclei.

Still smaller amebas live inside the human body. *Endamoeba coli* seems to be a harmless inhabitant of the intestine, where it feeds on bacteria. A majority of people have *E. gingivalis* policing the gum line around their teeth in a similar way. But if *E. histolytica* gains entry, as it can in contaminated water or food, it attacks the cells lining the intestine as an insidious parasite; the symptoms are those of amebiasis or amebic dysentery and are harder to cure than to avoid

23

(by boiling all drinking water and eating only cooked foods in regions where sanitation is questionable).

A shore-based naturalist is less likely to encounter the marine relatives of amebas, for both the members of order Foraminifera (the "forams") which produce a chambered shell (usually of lime and as much as 1/5 inch in diameter) and those of order Radiolaria (the "radiolarians") which support themselves on radiating spines of silica, are abundant only in the open sea far from land. In fresh water these protozoans have a few less impressive kin: the tiny sun animalcules, such as *Actinophrys* whose delicate, radiating pseudopodia resemble a sunburst but serve mostly as a trap for bacteria; and the little bowl amebas *(Arcella)* which extend lobe-shaped pseudopodia from the single opening of a circular, bowl-shaped shell composed of siliceous prisms cemented together by a protein material.

The Sporozoans (Class Sporozoa)

These protozoans are all internal parasites of larger animals and lack any means of moving from place to place on their own. As is indicated by the name of the class, they are spore-producing animals; after sexual fusion of sporozoan cells in pairs, they undergo multiple internal divisions to produce large numbers of infective units called sporozoites ("little animal spores").

The best known sporozoans are those of genus *Plasmodium*, the sporozoites of which get into man from an infected mosquito of the genus *Anopheles*. They travel through the blood stream to the human liver and reproduce there for a few days. Then they spread to the circulating blood and begin attacking red blood cells. A parasite enters a blood cell, grows while destroying the contents, multiplies inside the emptied red cell, providing a dozen new infective individuals that break out and attack still more red cells to repeat the process. The supply of intact red cells diminishes, causing an anemia, before the person develops an uncertain immunity. Before this stage is reached, the infected individual suffers repeated bouts of fever and chills, due apparently to wastes freed into the blood as new generations of parasites break out of the red cells on an almost synchronous schedule.

The hot skin of a person fevered by malaria attracts mosquitoes, which pick up the infection along with a blood meal. It is within the body of the infected mosquito that the parasite goes through sexual reproductive stages and forms the sporozoites that will migrate to the salivary glands of the insect. There the

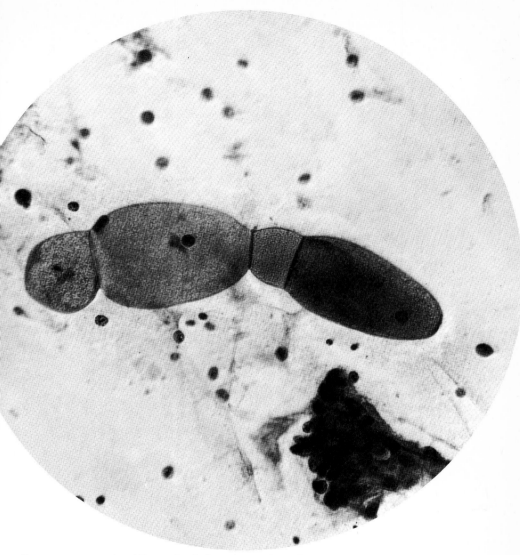

Sporozoan parasite (Gregarina) from insect intestine

sporozoites wait, ready to enter the next person the mosquito bites. The name malaria was given centuries ago when people credited this disease with coming from bad air, chiefly at night in summer where the land was low and marshy. The disease disappeared from Boston, London, and Moscow as wet places were filled in for urban construction long before 1901 when mosquitoes were discovered to transmit malaria. Now there is essentially no malaria for the *Anopheles* mosquitoes to transmit in the United States and Canada. The few cases discovered each year can usually be traced to exposure to infected mosquitoes during foreign travel, or to blood transfusions from a donor who was exposed at some time.

Related species of *Plasmodium* carried by *Culex* mosquitoes cause malarias in mammals other than man and birds. The "malaria" of waterfowl comes from members of genus *Leucocytozoon* and often kills 50 per cent or more of a year's hatch of young ducks, geese, and swans before they can develop an immunity. Blackflies *(Simulium)* transfer the infection. In the American Southwest, Texas cattle fever is sometimes equally devastating where ticks transfer the sporozoites of *Babesia bigemina*. Still other sporozoans are involved in coccidiosis of poultry, and in diseases that affect rabbits, dogs, cats, and familiar insects. Even earthworms have sporozoan diseases.

The Ciliates (Class Ciliata)

A somewhat larger size and faster movements make members of this class more conspicuous than other protozoans in fresh and salt waters. Ciliates often propel themselves several times their own length in a second or two. They travel through the surrounding liquid by the rhythmic activity of short hairlike projections called cilia (from the Latin *cilium*, an eyelash). The cilia arise in longitudinal or spiral rows, projecting from the flexible membrane, the pellicle, that covers the cell and reinforces its distinctive shape. Just inside the pellicle the cilia are linked by a communication network of fibrils which serve as a primitive nervous system. Other specializations within the cell demonstrate a division of labor analogous to that between the organ systems of multicellular animals. For this reason, the scientists who study ciliates often refer to them as acellular rather than cellular or unicellular.

Common ciliates in semistagnant water include several that are big enough to be recognized with no more than a hand lens to aid the eye. Popular names have been given to several, such as the slipper animalcules *(Paramecium)*, trumpet animalcules *(Stentor)*, and bell animalcules *(Vorticella)*. Although colorless, slipper animalcules, 1/100 inch long, can be detected with the unaided eye if light is reflecting off them more than from the dark bottom of a pool. Seen within the limited field of a compound microscope, they dart about at a magnified pace and become hard to follow. Yet patient observers have noticed that a

Paramecium gathers bacteria into a spherical cluster and then pushes the whole cluster (perhaps 1,000 bacteria) through a small opening in its pellicle as a food vacuole to be digested inside the cell. Repeating this process every six minutes or so, a slipper animalcule can double its own size in about 22 hours. In the pattern that is characteristic of ciliates, the cell then divides transversely to form two new identical individuals, each able to grow independently.

Trumpet animalcules, 1/25 inch long, may engulf euglenas and other small flagellates faster than one per second. The predatory ciliates do not restrict themselves to prey smaller than themselves. The barrel-shaped *Didinium* attacks slipper animalcules twice its volume; its oral pore through the pellicle stretches enough to engulf part of its prey. The remainder is taken in as quickly as digestive action can liquefy the victim.

The arrangement of the cilia, the shape of the whole cell, and the details of its inner structures, called organelles, vary greatly among the different kinds of ciliates. Yet a majority of them are free-living and found most abundantly where shallow water is well supplied with organic debris. When a bell animalcule finds a region with plenty of food, it usually attaches itself temporarily by means of a slender stalklike portion of the cell. This stalk region coils like a spiral spring, yanking the ciliated body portion toward the support and then pushing it out again to feed. These antics may create small local water currents that bring more food.

Members of the order Suctorida swim freely only when young; they lose their cilia after they attach themselves permanently. In place of locomotor structures, the suctorian extends coarse tentacles, some tipped with rounded knobs and some sharp pointed. The former are used to catch and hold small ciliates and other prey while the sharp tentacles pierce the victim and suck out its soft internal parts. Freshwater suctorians, such as *Podophrya* and *Tokophrya*, reproduce for a while by crosswise division and then by the repeated formation of small "buds" as immature individuals that are freed, develop cilia and swim away. Meanwhile, the mature "parent" remains attached, growing older and slower and eventually dying from internal deterioration.

The most complex inner structure is shown by peculiar ciliates such as *Epidinium* (formerly called *Diplodinium*) which live in the paunch of cud-chewing mammals, including cattle, sheep, goats and antelopes. A mature beef animal may contain 10 to 50 billion of these ciliates, which digest particles of the food the cud-chewer eats and seems not to harm it in any way.

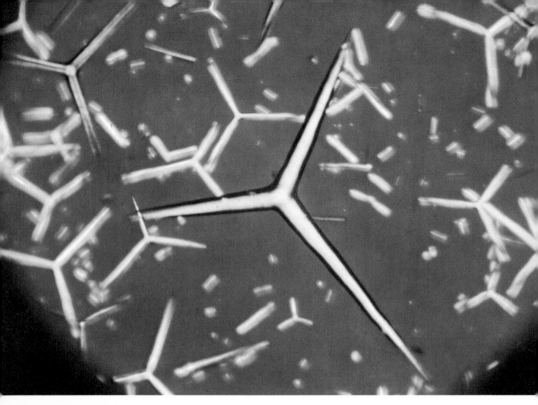

Spicules from skeleton of Calcareous Sponge (Leuconia)

The Sponges *(Phylum Porifera)*

Sponges are all aquatic members of the Animal Kingdom. They live attached to rocks and other solid objects. Only the members of one family occur in fresh water; all other sponges are marine. To be convinced that sponges are animals rather than plants requires that a living specimen be examined with a microscope. The minute pores, for which the phylum is named "the pore bearers," that mark the surface are too small to see otherwise. Their presence might be assumed from a simple experiment. If a small quantity of harmless dye is introduced into the water close to the sponge, the color simply vanishes into the inert-appearing mass and reappears only from the conspicuous openings on its surface. No wonder the Greeks used their word *sphongos* for both a sponge and a fungus, the one in water, the other on land. Even the name for the conspicuous openings, oscula, meaning "little mouths," gives the wrong

28

impression since water and wastes are discharged from them and nothing important to the sponge enters there.

Sponges vary greatly in shape, size, color, and texture. Yet each one is a cooperating society of cells that temporarily assume some one of four different forms—and later change places and roles in the colony. At any particular time a cell may be somewhat flattened and abut others like it as a surface cell, helping maintain a boundary around the colony. Or it may be a pore cell, shaped like a doughnut with a hole right through its center; in this case, it will be located where it can admit water from the outside world into some branch of the system of spaces inside the colony, which open at the exhalant oscula. The cell may be situated where it can extend a single flagellum, surrounded by a flexible collar of cytoplasm (making it a "collar cell"), into one of the branching, water-filled spaces. Collar cells use their flagella to create a current of water in through the pore cells and out through the oscula. Their cytoplasmic collars capture bacteria and other particles of food from the water as it passes them. The cell may resemble an ameba and move about between the collar cells and the others in the colony, picking up food vacuoles from the collar cells and distributing them so that all cells get nourishment. Frequently the ameboid cells come together in little groups and secrete skeletal materials that both support the sponge and also repel carnivorous animals.

The fine details of the skeleton in a sponge seem to offer scientists the most reliable clues for telling one kind from another. Even the primary division of the phylum into classes follows these distinctions.

The Calcareous or Limy Sponges (Class Calcarea)

These sponges secrete limy skeletal elements, which may be needle-like or 3- or 4-branched. The coasts of North America have a number of representatives, principally from Cape Cod northward to the Arctic along the Atlantic side and in similarly cool waters on the Pacific shoreline. These sponges tend to be small, tubular or urn-shaped, with a bristly surface and dull colors. A branching system of interconnected stolons, which adhere closely to the surface of some shady stone or rock wall in shallow water or a tidal pool, may give rise to erect fingerlike bodies 1/8 inch to 1-1/4 inches tall. A thin wall around the central cavity and no distinctive features around the circular osculum at the unattached end help identify a member of *Leucosolenia*. Calcareous sponges with a thicker wall and a flaring end around the osculum are usually *Scypha*.

Overleaf: left, Sulfur Sponge (Verongia thiona) and small anemones; top right, Freshwater Sponge colony (Spongilla); right center, Free-rolling Bun Sponge (Tetilla mutabilis); bottom right, Blue Sponge

The Glass Sponges (Class Hexactinellida)

A beachcomber is unlikely to find a glass sponge because these animals rarely live in water less than 30 feet deep or where storms will wash them loose and toss them ashore. Their bodies lack any covering layer of flat cells and their collar cells are clumped in small groups well concealed within a meshwork of glass skeletal elements. These hard parts may be either 6-rayed, mere needles, short rods with a circlet of hooks at each end, or hairlike fibers so long that they can anchor the whole sponge erect in mud on the sea floor. Skin divers sometimes find examples of the glass rope sponge *(Hyalonema)* off the New England coast between 30 and 45 feet deep. Farther south and in the Gulf of Mexico, the depth limit for glass sponges is about 100 feet below the surface. Along the Pacific shoreline, they are sometimes dredged from water 60 feet or more in depth.

The Siliceous and Horny Sponges (Class Demospongiae)

Most sponges that are encountered along the sea coast, whether alive or cast up by storms, belong to this class. A few genera seem strange in their lack of a skeleton of any kind. Others have siliceous spicules that are 4-rayed or needle-like, but never 6-rayed. The most common sponges have needle-like spicules and spongin too. They include the sulfur sponge *(Suberites)* that often grows on snail shells that are carried about by hermit crabs. It attains more massive size on rocks. The yellow to yellow-gray color of the sulfur sponge gives it a superficial resemblance to the cosmopolitan boring sponge *(Cliona)* that attaches itself to limestone and to the shells of live snails and bivalves. The boring sponge dissolves pits and cavities into both types of support until the limestone surface crumbles and the mollusk shells disintegrate. By destroying their shells, the sponge dooms the mollusks and makes shellfisheries much less productive. The sponge itself may outlive the collapse of its support, however, by breaking into fragments, which are redistributed by water movements, become reattached and grow elsewhere.

The breadcrumb sponge *(Halichondria)* often produces colorful carpets over rocks and the floors of tide pools, with a velvety surface in green to yellow to orange-brown that is raised at intervals in little cones with an osculum at the tip. A similar encrustment of the redbeard sponge *(Microciona)* along either the Atlantic or the Pacific coast may be bright red to orange brown. It supports a large number of upright branching fingers wherever it grows in subtidal waters. Related species in deeper waters around the Gulf of Mexico tend to be paler in color; when torn loose by a storm and cast upon the beach, where they bleach in the sun, they are known as "dead man's fingers."

The only sponges in fresh waters belong to the family Spongillidae, with *Spongilla* the commonest of about 15 genera; these include approximately 150 species. They are widespread in slow streams, ponds, and lakes across the continent, growing as irregular coatings on submerged tree branches, stones or even living plants. Occasionally, a colony a foot across is found where the water level changes little all year. Some are bright green, and others a dull olive-brown. Apparently all of them maintain between their cells minute green algae, which carry on photosynthesis and contribute to the welfare of the sponge. As an adaptation to the dual hazards of desiccation during droughts and freezing in winter, the freshwater sponges produce internal buds called gemmules, which are freed when the sponge dies and decomposes. The gemmules bear a dense coating of spicules around all surfaces and tolerate loss of water and severe cold. They survive adverse conditions and often ride from one region to another on the feet of wading birds. Under suitable conditions, the gemmules burst open and the cells start the growth of a new sponge.

Commercial sponges are the carefully prepared remains of horny sponges. These members of the subclass Keratosa have no spicules, and only a skeleton of spongin fibers. Most are rounded colonies with a blackish leathery surface through which irregular oscula open from extensive cavities inside. The valuable kinds that were harvested by sponge divers in the Gulf of Mexico and Caribbean Sea prior to 1939 grew on rocky outcrops, reefs, and dead corals close to muddy bottoms, where bacteria apparently was abundant and served as food. The sponge fishery, which was centered in Tarpon Springs and Key West, collapsed when a fungus *(Spongiophaga communis)* caused widespread and intensive mortality among the most-sought species of *Euspongia* and *Hippospongia*. The euspongias are often called "bath sponges"; they include species known to the trade as grass sponges, glove sponges, Florida yellow sponges, and hardheads. The hippospongias or "horse sponges" include the commercial sheepswool and the velvet sponge.

Since the populations of valuable sponges have never regained their former numbers, despite the virtual cessation of fishing for them, scientists wonder what else caused the decline. No change has been noticed in the abundance of other horny sponges, whose remains are often cast up on Florida beaches. These

Vase Sponge (Hircina sp.)

include the branching vase sponge *(Callyspongia vaginalis)* whose oscula at the branch ends are often large enough to admit a thumb, and whose lumpy surfaces becomes pale gray in the sun. The solitary vase sponge *(Hircina)*, which ranges up the Atlantic coast as far as Virginia as well as around the Gulf of Mexico, forms an open cone in which a fair-sized grapefruit could be hidden. The living vase sponges are attached in deep water well off shore. Those a beachcomber finds have lost all of their living cells and many of the finer cross connecting fibers in the network of spongin. In this respect they resemble the fine-textured commercial sponges that have been killed by exposure to air, let rot in the sun, been rinsed thoroughly with fresh water and frequently beaten to free any snail shells or other hard particles from the inner chambers.

A spectacular array of small animals do take up residence on and in sponges. This is often discovered by a skin diver who has found, in the warm shallows where tidal currents flow between the Florida Keys, a loggerhead sponge *(Ircinia strobilina)* as big as a medicine ball. If the sponge is brought ashore and cut open, small crabs, amphipod crustaceans, snapping shrimps, mantis shrimps, worms, and serpent stars drop out. Periwinkles and other snails find holes in which to hide. Barnacles may be embedded in the sponge surface. Even moss animals (bryozoans) and colonial tunicates sometimes have attached themselves. Algae often grow on the sponge. Yet few of these commensal species seem to get anything from the sponge except support and concealment. Judging by the size of the loggerhead sponge, the invaders do not do much harm.

During the few minutes of slack water when a particularly low tide has fully ebbed, any large sponge in a shallow tidal gutter may be seen to be producing a current of its own. Jets emerge from its many oscula, roiling the water. Measurements show that a loggerhead sponge a foot in diameter can circulate a ton of water through its pore cells and branching spaces every day. From this volume, its collar cells may pick up an ounce of food particles such as bacteria. At the same time, the in-and-out current maintained by the myriad beating flagella brings oxygen and carries away wastes. The sponge engulfs ameboid cells that will serve as sperm; captured by the collar cells in another sponge of the same species, these sperm burrow into the colony and fuse with other ameboid cells that are acting as eggs. Soon small embryos emerge in the outgoing water current, each helping propel itself by the beating of flagella on its surface cells. Then each embryo settles, rearranges its cells to move those with flagella inside, and starts operating as a typical sponge. Apparently this same extraordinarily simple way of life has been successful with minor changes during more than 600 million years, for sponge skeletal elements are found as fossils in Pre-Cambrian strata.

The Nettle-cell Bearers
(Phylum Cnidaria or Coelenterata)

Aristotle called them sea-nettles and distinguished between two types. One "clings to rocks. . . . It has no shell, but its entire body is fleshy. It is sensitive to touch and, if you put your hand to it, it will seize and cling to it . . . and in such a way as to make the flesh of your hand swell up. Its mouth is in the center of its body, and it lives adhering to the rock as an oyster to its shell. . . . The sea-nettle appears to be devoid altogether of excretion, and in this respect it resembles a plant." We call these cylindrical creatures polyps, and call the most conspicuous ones sea anemones. The other type is saucer-shaped and, as Aristotle said, it "roams freely abroad." We call it a jellyfish or a medusa.

The ability of these aquatic animals to cling and sting and their underlying radial symmetry sets them apart from other forms of life. The Greek word *knide*, which Aristotle used for a sea-nettle, was revived for the phylum Cnidaria. It is used again in cnidoblast ("nettle cell") for the distinctive type of cell found in the surface layer of every cnidarian, arming it for clinging and stinging, for capturing food and defending itself. No other cell in the Animal Kingdom matures by forming inside its outer end a minute egg-shaped capsule containing a coiled thread tube. When ready to fire, it responds independently to chemical substances diffusing through the water from small animals upon which the cnidarian usually feeds. Explosively the thread is everted, injecting a fluid that can paralyze a victim or enable it to cling to it and prevent it from escaping. The cnidoblasts are most numerous on the slender tentacles that each cnidarian extends like flexible fishing poles.

The difference between an attached polyp and a free-swimming medusa is not as fundamental as the differences in behavior suggest. Both forms of cnidarian have an outer layer of cells forming an epidermal tissue, and an inner tissue (the endodermis) associated with the saclike central digestive cavity. This cavity, which is commonly dilated by the water and food it contains, is the basis for the alternate name of the phylum, the Coelenterata (literally, "body cavity a gut"). The two tissues meet at the mouth, through which food is taken into the digestive cavity and undigested wastes are spat out.

Between the two tissues of a cnidarian is a layer of noncellular secretion called the mesoglea ("middle jelly"). It provides most of the thickness of a jellyfish, but is thin in the body of the more muscular polyps. A polyp is simply attached by glandular secretions at the end of its body farthest from its mouth. A medusa swims about feebly by expelling water from the concave side of its saucer-shaped body, past its mouth, which is at the end of a dangling central projection. The tentacles on a medusa arise around the rim of its body, whereas those on a polyp originate in a circle closer to the mouth. In either case, when food is caught by a tentacle or two, it is brought to the mouth and pushed into the central digestive cavity. There digestion begins, causing the prey to disintegrate into fragments. The small fragments are then taken into cells of the endodermis in food vacuoles where the process is completed.

About a third of the known kinds of cnidarians are placed in the Class Hydrozoa because of their relatively simple body structure and their pattern of individual development. Ordinarily their fertilized eggs come from small medusae, but develop into solitary or colonial polyps which reproduce asexually

Freshwater Hydra (Chlorohydra sp.)

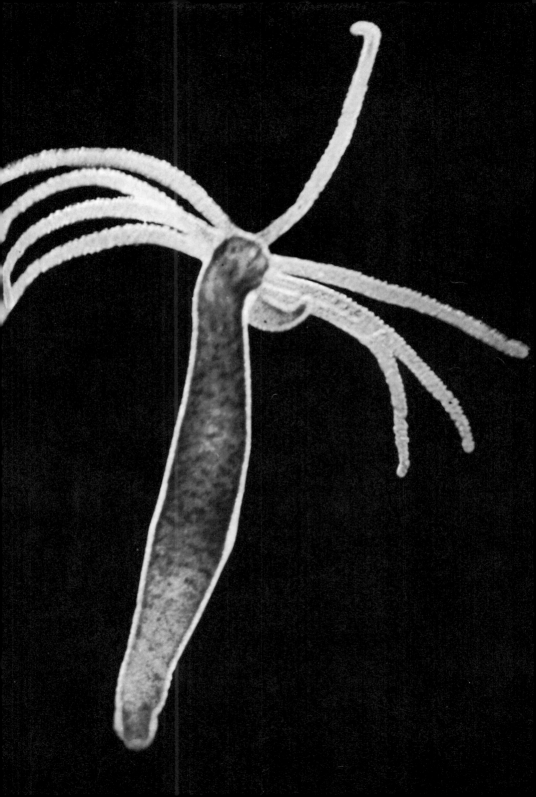

by budding for a while and then liberate small medusae. Members of Class Scyphozoa are relatively few. They are larger medusae and the development of the polyp stage is lacking or much reduced. Members of Class Anthozoa outnumber in variety all other cnidarians; they are the corals, the sea anemones and their kin. The polyps are more complex in structure and they reproduce with no medusa stage.

The Hydrozoan Polyps and Medusae (Class Hydrozoa)

Most hydrozoans live in shallow salt waters. Yet their class name ("hydra animals") and the word hydroid ("hydra-like"), which is used often in place of polyp for the attached individuals, relate to some peculiar members of the class that inhabit fresh water. These transparent freshwater polyps received the name *Hydra* in reference to the many-headed monster in Greek mythology and to some experiments described in 1744 by the Swiss naturalist Abraham Trembley. He believed he had found animals that were potentially immortal. When he cut the half-inch cylindrical body of a freshwater polyp into pieces, each quickly regenerated into a whole new individual. When he divided a polyp part way down from the mouth toward the base, where it was attached, it healed in a "Y" shape, with a mouth and complete set of tentacles at each of the diverging free ends. These too he divided part way, and soon had a monster to feed.

A freshwater polyp produces side branches from its main stalklike body. Each branch develops its own mouth and tentacles while its central digestive cavity is still connected to that of its parent and, through it, the side branch (a "bud") shares captured food in both directions. In a few days, however, the bud is likely to separate and move away on its own. Like adult hydras, it may glide along gradually on its own adhesive substance, or it may perform slow somersaults by bending and holding to the substratum with its tentacles while the end farthest from the mouth comes free and reaches in a new direction to affix itself again.

Freshwater crustaceans form the principal food of hydras. Occasionally a big brown hydra *(Pelmatohydra oligactis)*, 3/4 inch long, manages to capture and engulf a very small tadpole. Sometimes thousands of cnidarians manage to get started in the rearing tanks and troughs at fish hatcheries and there dine on hatchling fishes. Larger fishes in ponds and streams find hydras edible and snatch them from the underside of waterlily pads.

Hydras are quite widespread in fresh waters across North America, without

Preceding page: Ostrich-plume Hydroids (Aglaophenia sp.)

having to creep or somersault or swim there on their own. Unlike hydroids in salt water, *Hydra* and its close kin produce no medusas. Instead they develop sex organs in the epidermis of the polyp stalk. Sperms are freed into the water, but eggs are held until they are fertilized and an embryo has grown considerably. Protected within a drought and cold resistant covering, it drops out into the water where, if conditions are suitable, the embryo hatches and takes on the form of a young hydra after a dormant period of 10 to 70 days. Until it hatches, however, the embryo in its covering can become embedded in mud on the feet of a wading bird, and ride along as potential colonist to some distant body of water; it may be a fish hatchery, a bird bath or a swimming pool. The young hydra will survive better if chance places it where prey of suitable size is abundant.

Along sea coasts the corresponding hydrozoans are far more varied. Like the freshwater hydras, most are the members of the order Anthomedusae, which mostly produce little medusae less than 1/8 inch in diameter, bearing sex organs along the sides of the stalk that bears the mouth. The hydroid stages are soft, and sometimes form velvety coverings from 1/8 to 1 inch deep over pilings or on coarse seaweeds. Virtually unsupported except by buoyancy, they collapse and often die if exposed by a receding tide. When covered by calm water, they sway and extend their tentacles to capture minute prey. Details that a specialist can discern in any polyp distinguish the colonies of *Bougainvillea*, *Eudendrium*, *Tubularia*, and other genera. The hedgehog hydroid *(Hydractinia)*, which often encrusts the snail shells that hermit crabs are carrying around, gets its common name from the spiny mat formed by the basal parts that unite members of the colony.

A second order, the Leptomedusae, includes animals that similarly appear in two guises. But the medusae, which are generally more flattened, wear the sex organs along the four radial canals that mark off the saucer-shaped body, and the polyp stages encase themselves in a transparent chitinous sheath except where the tentacles reach out for food or where the young medusae are released. The sheath provides extra support and allows the hydroid colonies to form feathery branches as much as 12 inches long. They yield to water movements while keeping the interconnected polyps spread out, their tentacles reaching for food in a fair sample of the environment.

One of the most conspicuous of the colonial hydroids gives a scuba diver the impression that shrubby white heather is growing on the sea floor at depths to about 50 feet. The "plant" bears the common name of whiteweed in England; elsewhere in its range from the English Channel to the Arctic and down the

Overleaf: top left, Pacific Coast Medusa (Pelagia); bottom left, underneath side of Medusa; right, Atlantic Coast Medusa (Chrysaora quinquecirrha)

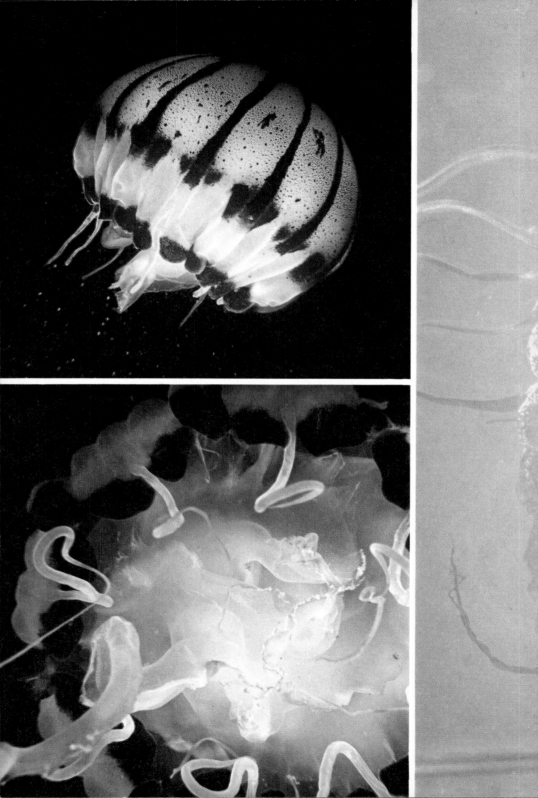

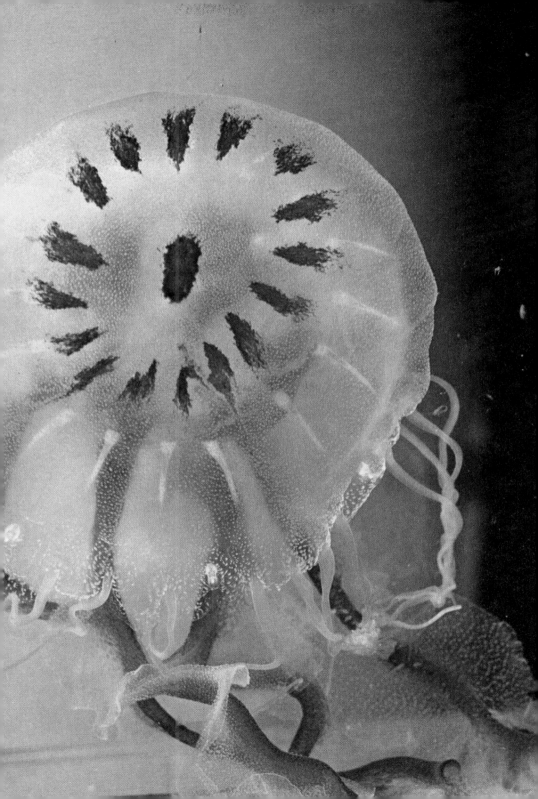

North American coast from Labrador to Cape Hatteras scientists know it as *Thuiaria argentea*. It is the basis for a small industry along the English coast, where men collect it, clean, dye and dry the branches, then ship them to the United States for sale in flower shops and supermarkets as "sea ferns." As advertised, the flexible sheaths last for years, stay green without watering, and never outgrow the pot in which they are placed. The tiny bell-shaped cups that once protected living polyps can be seen along both sides of each branch by anyone who examines the "fern" with a good magnifier.

The distinctive features of each species of hydroid are easier to recognize under a microscope. In some, such as *Thuiaria*, *Sertularia*, and *Obelia*, the individual polyps seem to rest directly upon the graceful branches of the colony. In others, such as *Campanularia* and *Clytia*, each polyp is at the end of its own long slender stalk or secondary branch. Often the shape of the enclosures and the arrangement of polyps on the branches reveal specific differences that might not be guessed at from examination of the soft parts of the animal itself.

Most members of the orders Leptomedusae and Anthomedusae are found near shore, in relatively shallow water. Seemingly, the ciliated larvae (planulas) that develop from the fertilized eggs of the medusa stage must not have too far to swim or sink before reaching the bottom, where they can attach themselves and start new colonies of hydroids. This limitation seems to have been bypassed in other hydrozoans. Those in order Hydrocorallina, which include the stinging coral *(Millepora)* of warm coasts of Florida and the Gulf of Mexico, omit the medusa stage; the minute polyps protrude from pores in a massive limy skeleton. Stinging coral, whose nettling cells produce a particularly powerful venom, is hard to recognize because it comes in many colors and often conforms to the dead corals, sea fans and other objects it encrusts, showing few identifying features of its own. The members of the order Trachelina have evolved in the opposite direction, by reducing or obliterating the hydroid stage, whereas those of order Siphonophora keep all stages together in a single complex colony that swims or drifts without reference to the sea floor.

Until the 1930's, when the eelgrass died off so catastrophically around the world, New Englanders used to see large numbers of the trachyline medusa *Gonionemus vertens*. The 4/5-inch transparent bells have a cross-shaped marking in the dome, produced by the ruffled sex organs. Now these medusae are less common. They swim feebly in saltwater ponds or cling by means of special knobs on their tentacles to waving leaves of eelgrass where it grows again; the medusae reproduce without hydroid stages. The close relative *Craspedacusta*

Portuguese Man-of-War (Physalia pelagica)

sowerbyi lives in fresh water and does have a diminutive hydroid to which the name *Microhydra* was given before the complete life history became known. The greenish polyps, 1/8-inch high with a few tentacles, produce medusae from buds. Apparently the polyps also survive being carried from place to place in mud on the feet of wading birds. No other explanation has been discovered for the appearance and disappearance of freshwater medusae in almost every state

Overleaf: left, Shrubby Gorgonian; top right, Gorgonian (Muricea); bottom right, Branching Red Gorgonian and Purple Hydrocoral (Allopora Porphyra)

and province of North America and on other continents as well. They inhabit slow rivers, remote ponds and occasionally alarm people who find medusae in their swimming pools.

Best known of the colonial siphonophores is the Portuguese man-of-war *(Physalia pelagica)*. Each colony consists of at least four kinds of polyps: one has the extraordinary ability to secrete gas within itself until it becomes a living balloon, keeping the colony afloat and to some extent regulating the direction it will move when blown by the wind. Feeding polyps of a brilliant blue color, with a terminal mouth and one or more long blue tentacles, dangle beneath the float, waiting for a fish, crustacean or other victim to get caught and paralyzed by the stinging cells. Food is shared by the feeding polyps with each other, with the float individual, and with both the fingerlike green polyps that surrounded the colony and the salmon-pink reproductive polyps toward the center of the under surface. Portuguese man-of-wars are well known in tropical seas and the Gulf of Mexico. They often ride the Gulf Stream all the way to Europe. Many are blown ashore along Atlantic coasts. Large colonies of this kind have a float 14 inches long and contractile tentacles reaching 60 feet or more into the water below. They are dangerous to human swimmers, because the poison in the stinging cells is one of the most powerful known among marine animals. Even a small, dead man-of-war on the beach can give a painful sting to a bare foot. Fortunately, the ghost crabs drag the man-of-wars to their burrows and pull them below, apparently immune to the venom.

The Larger Medusae (Class Scyphozoa)

Almost any medusa more than 2 inches in diameter is a member of this class. Some, such as the pink jelly known as the "lion's mane" *(Cyanea arctica)*, attain a width of 12 inches south of Cape Cod but continue to grow in colder waters until, in the Arctic, they reach 8 feet across. The 800 tentacles of this animal do not hang from the rim of the bell but from a circular zone on the underside. On a 3-foot specimen the tentacles may extend 75 feet below and behind the medusa, while on an 8-footer a length of 200 feet would not be unusual. In virulence and number the stinging cells on even a 12-inch lion's mane make it formidable and capable of incapacitating the strongest human swimmer, causing him to drown. Yet young whitings, and perhaps other commercial fish too, seem to gain protection from predators by associating with Atlantic members of this wide-spread species.

Scyphozoans all possess extra tentacles around the mouth, and produce their sex organs in the lining of the central digestive cavity rather than from epidermis below the bell. In the common moon jelly *(Aurelia)*, the corners of the mouth are extended into four long tapering ribbonlike structures, each V-shaped in section with hundreds of fine short tentacles concealed in the V. The body may be 10 to 12 inches across, like a semitransparent ghostly form swimming up to the surface and then down again, with a pattern of four ring-shaped reproductive organs more opaque and either pale pink (male) or shining white (female). In *Cassiopeia*, which is common in the Gulf of Mexico and around the tip of Florida, the mouth region seems massive and frilly. Actually it is subdivided, providing the animal with many mouths. Often members of this genus lie on their backs on the muddy or sandy bottom of shallow bays, scarcely moving as they capture food from the gentle current of water that flows across them. By contrast, *Stomolophus meleagris* propels its firm, honey-colored, 7-inch body with special vigor, its multiple mouths dangling from the center of the mushroom-shaped bell. It inhabits the same tropical waters, ranging up the Atlantic coast to the Carolinas and up the Pacific coast to San Diego.

The Sea Anemones and Their Kin (Class Anthozoa or Actinozoa)

The class name signifies "flower animals." It refers to the most conspicuous and influential group of cnidarians, many of which have been producing great reefs for hundreds of millions of years. All of these animals are marine polyps or colonies of polyps, living in relatively shallow water. Sea anemones and sea pens do move about slowly under their own power when living conditions deteriorate, but the soft corals, horny corals (including sea whips and sea fans), and the stony corals live permanently attached. They are dispersed by little free-swimming larvae (planulas) which can be carried long distances by ocean currents. Anthozoans differ from hydrozoans in having the digestive cavity divided lengthwise by partitions and the mesoglea somewhat organized—almost enough to be called a connective tissue. The soft corals and horny corals are placed in one subclass (the Octocorallia) because they have 8 partitions and 8 pinnately branched tentacles and produce whatever skeletal materials support them between the epidermis and the lining layer of the digestive cavity. Stony corals, by contrast, secrete a limy skeleton outside the body; like sea anemones they have few to many tentacles (never 8), 6 partitions (or some multiple) in

Overleaf: left, Sea Fan in a coral garden; right, Sea Pens (Stylatula)

the digestive cavity, and are placed in the second subclass (the Hexacorallia).

Except in the warm waters of the subtropics and tropics, almost no octocorals grow in shallows where an explorer with face plate and snorkel can see them. At higher latitudes, some kinds live at greater depths where they get caught on the deep nets of fishermen or can be collected with special sampling dredges. Around the tip of Florida, however, and in a few places elsewhere along the shores of the Gulf of Mexico, the sea whips (*Eunicea*, *Plexaura*, and others), sea plumes (such as *Antillogorgia acerosa*) and sea fans *(Gorgonia flabellum)* live just beyond easy reach. They can be watched waving with the currents but stay in place because the short main trunk from which the branches arise is expanded into intimate contact with some firm object in or on the sea floor. The conspicuous parts of these colonial animals are stiffened with limy spicules while a secretion of hornlike gorgonin provides lengthwise strength. In a sea whip, the gorgonin is concentrated in the central core, whereas in a sea plume it

Sea Pansy (Renilla kollikeri)

enters also the side branches of the colony, and in a sea fan helps form the flat latticework which may be four feet tall, more than two feet wide, and mostly less than 1/8 inch thick.

By day, the minute polyps that dot the surfaces of these gorgonians tend to pull in their eight feathery tentacles and disappear. At night they are fully expanded and capture food from the water that moves past. No one need fear to brush against a sea whip or sea fan, for its stinging cells are too minute and weak in venom to affect human skin. But the polyps retract at the slightest touch, and often if too bright a flashlamp beam is turned in their direction.

South of Cape Hatteras, around the Gulf of Mexico, and in protected bays of California where the sun warms the cold waters of the Pacific Ocean, muddy shorelines are sometimes littered with sea pansies *(Renilla)* that have been washed out by a storm. From a boat they can often be seen like slightly convex pieces of a mosaic floor, imbedded side by side in the sediments with just their

Sea Pen (Leioptilus guerneyi)

Stony Coral Polyp (Balanophyllia elegans)

Preceding page: Red Sea Anemones (Corynactis californica)

purple tops exposed. Each top is densely set with feeding polyps, while the "stalk" of the sea pansy reduces the chance that a wave will flip it free. At night, these creatures luminesce with a soft bluish light if disturbed in any way. So do the feathery sea pens (green *Stylatula* and flesh-colored *Acanthoptilum*) in similar shallows between San Diego and San Francisco, unless the stimulus frightens them into pulling their exposed parts into the sandy mud. If the 20-inch sea pens *(Pennatula)* that halibut fishermen sometimes bring up from the edge of the Atlantic continental shelf have similar habits, no beachcomber is likely to find out. No matter how common an animal may be at depths greater than 600 feet, its privacy from prolonged human observation is at present insured.

Sea anemones are much easier to find. Many live in tide pools and may keep their tentacles expanded so long as water covers them. Or they may tuck every tentacle into the mouth and resemble only a pastel-colored fleshy fruit, such as a plum or peach, that has had the end cut off and then been stuck firmly to the rock. The body of the anemone feels rubbery when nudged, but only an individual that is exposed is likely to retract.

From New Jersey to the Arctic, and down the European coast in cool water, the commonest large sea anemone is *Metridium senile*, whose velvet-smooth body, 4 inches tall, ends in a wavy oral disc 3 inches across, surrounded by hundreds of short fine tentacles. The animal may be any color from white to chocolate-brown, plain or blotched, and obviously single or in the slow process of reproducing asexually. In this, the body may divide lengthwise into two of almost equal size, or a bud may grow out of the side as though the process could be as simple as in a hydra despite all the partitions inside the digestive cavity. Or a lump may separate from the flaring base and reorganize itself as a small anemone of the same kind.

On cool coasts of the Pacific Ocean, the same *Metridium* is less common than the green *Anthopleura xanthogrammica*, whose flat oral disc does not fold well enough for the tentacles to be concealed. These animals, with bits of sand and shell often sticking to their outer surfaces, hold to positions on coastal rocks where they are exposed to air and even sun for hours at each low tide. Their green color is due to algal cells in the depths of the epidermis, where photosynthesis may provide the anemone with some extra nourishment as well as absorbing the carbon dioxide from its respiration.

Almost cosmopolitan now is the little green or brown (often striped orange, yellow, white) anemone *Haliplanella luciae*, 1/2 to 3/4 inch tall, with 20 to

Left, Tentacles around the mouth of a Giant Red Sea Amenome (Tealia crassicornis); bottom left, Giant Red Sea Anemone, side view; bottom center, Red Sea Anemone (Tealia lofotensis) feeding on Sea Star (Patiria miniata); bottom right, Tube Dwelling Sea Anemone (Cerianthus eastuari) withdrawn to safety

50 long slender tentacles. It lives on pilings, or among mussels, and often invades brackish water to find a place in salt marshes. First noticed at New Haven, Connecticut, in 1892, it probably came from Japan in the bilges of a ship. Now it is widespread around the North Atlantic coasts, frequent in the Gulf of Mexico, and well known in and near many Pacific ports. Older descriptions refer it to the genus *Sagartia* or *Aipaisiomorpha*.

A flaring base on a 3-inch anemone with short tentacles is characteristic of *Calliactis tricolor*, which often rides along on the backs of crabs and on snail shells that large hermit crabs carry. The same species associates in clusters on rocks below the low-tide line along the southern portion of the Atlantic coast and around the Gulf of Mexico. Probably the anemone gains tidbits from meals the crab (or hermit crab) is eating, and the crustacean gains protection from predators that avoid the stinging tentacles of the anemone. When hermit crabs change shells for a larger one, they gently pick off the anemone and position it on the new covering. The anemone responds to its associate, for it lets go promptly, whereas it resists any attempt to dislodge it with human fingers or a stick.

Stony corals have no need to distinguish among animals that are unsuitable as prey. Each coral animal is permanently attached within the cup of its limy secretion. Only one kind, the star coral *(Astrangia danae)*, is hardy enough to tolerate the cool waters close to shores of New England. It forms low branching growths on rocks, pilings and shells from the low-tide line to a depth of 120 feet. The individual polyps are less than 1/4 inch tall, translucent white or pinkish, with about two dozen short transparent tentacles, each raised in minute areas where the nettling cells are clustered. A similar species *(A. lajollaensis)* in tide pools of southern California is bright orange to coral-red, with white knobs tipping each of the pale tentacles.

The reef-forming corals live only where the water temperature in the coldest month is barely, if ever, below 70° F., and where daylight penetrates at intensities high enough to support photosynthesis. The coral animals themselves have no chlorophyll. Yet each one maintains within its tissues large numbers of minute algal cells and, in some way, gains from the activity of the plants. Without them the cnidarian cannot obtain the calcium it needs for its external support. Secretion of the lime takes place only by day and at rates that vary with the amount of sunlight. In the white limestone that accumulates progressively to form the reef, scientists have been able to find lines that record the days, the major storms, the seasonal changes with the years.

Fully a dozen different reef-forming corals are common around southern Florida and in the West Indies. Outliers live in the Gulf of Mexico. The most massive, such as *Montastrea annularis* at depths between 30 and 60 feet, are rarely seen except by scuba divers whose supplementary lights may reveal the yellowish brown color of the expanded polyps. Nearer the surface are rounded brain corals (*Diploria labyrinthiformis* and others), tropical star corals *(Favia)*, staghorns *(Acropora)* and delicate West Indian leaf corals *(Agaricia)*. Few of them live nearer the low-tide level than five feet down. But every storm breaks off pieces of the more fragile kinds and tosses them ashore. Many of these trophies tempt the beachcomber to get the equipment necessary to explore the reefs themselves. The living world offers few places that are richer in diverse animal life or more different from the familiar habitats on land.

The Comb-jellies *(Phylum Ctenophora)*

So glassy are the transparent bodies of most comb-jellies that their presence in coastal waters is often noticed only when sunlight reflects in iridescent colors from the tiny paddles in eight lengthwise rows as these animals propel themselves along. Seen in silhouette, the paddles suggest the teeth of a comb, hence the name ctenophore ("comb-bearer"), from the Greek *ctenos* meaning comb. Commonly, the body is almost spherical or egg-shaped. This form, and certainly not the delicate texture, is referred to in the common names of the few that are seen most often: sea gooseberries, sea walnuts, and sea thimbles.

For many years, comb-jellies were included along with the cnidarians in the phylum Coelenterata. But the ctenophores lack nettle cells, reproduce only by sexual means, have ameboid cells and muscle strands in the mesoglea that separates the epidermis from the cell layer lining the digestive cavity, and differ in other features that earn them a phylum of their own. All are carnivorous, eating from among the drifting plankton great numbers of larval worms, mollusks, and crustaceans, and sometimes taking an important toll of the eggs and young herrings, cod, and other fishes.

Almost a third of the 80 different kinds of comb-jellies in the world can be found along North American coasts. A few species are cosmopolitan, but rarely encountered in the tropical seas because at low latitudes they stay deeper, where the water temperature is comparable to that at the surface in spring and fall at middle latitudes and in summer closer to the poles. Other species are limited in distribution. The majority are small, between 1/5 and 4/5 inch long.

Sometimes a receding tide leaves many thousands of 4/5-inch sea goose-berries *(Pleurobrachia)* stranded where a beachcomber discovers them glittering in the light of early morning. If scooped up gently and placed in a pailful of sea water, they seem to disappear because they are so transparent. If placed, instead, in a small glass jar, a sea gooseberry can often be seen moving slowly, with two long slender arms waving at the sides. Each arm is equipped with special lasso cells, and able to catch, then transfer small items of food to the terminal mouth. Often the mouth and tentacles are faintly brownish, orange, yellow, or milky white. *P. pileus* shows a preference for cold waters in the north Atlantic and Pacific and around Antarctica; *P. brunnea*, which has a row of bright purple spots halfway down each tentacle, tolerates more warmth and is found from New Jersey south to the West Indies and around the Gulf of Mexico; *P. bachei* is often common along the Pacific coast from San Diego to Puget Sound.

The sea walnuts *(Mertensia)* may be 2 inches long and have a pear-shaped outline to the somewhat flattened, pinkish body. Two long tentacles with lasso cells show the relationship of these cretures to the sea gooseberries. On the Atlantic coast, *M. ovum* is sometimes common north of New Jersey, whereas different species range along the Pacific coast. Differences in shape and inner details distinguish *Hormiphora plumosa*, which glides through warm waters of the Gulf of Mexico, the tropical Atlantic Ocean and the Mediterranean Sea.

A two-lobed body and tentacles so short that they may be overlooked are characteristic of some larger comb-jellies that often ride the coastal currents past docks on which observant fishermen are watching the water. North of Cape Cod, a lobed ctenophore is most likely to be a *Bolinopsis infundibulum*. South of the Cape the members of *Mnemiopsis* are commoner, *M. leidyi* from Connecticut to the Carolinas, and *M. mccreadyi* from there to the West Indies and around the Gulf of Mexico; these animals sometimes grow to be 4 inches long and lack any widely popular name.

Venus's girdles, which are comb-jellies of genera *Cestum* and *Folia*, have an extraordinarily ribbonlike form and progress through the water in an undulating fashion near the surface or roll up and unroll repeatedly at greater depths. The comb plates that propel the animal form a double fringe along the edges of the ribbon, while the stomach and a few other organs are midway between the two ends. North of Cape Hatteras, *Folia parallela* is the principal Venus's girdle;

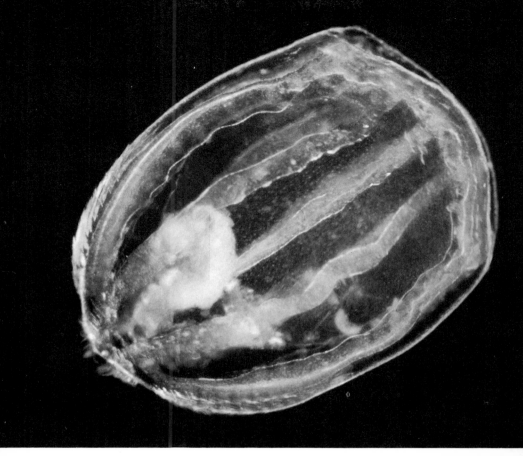

Comb-jelly (Beroë sp.)

it attains a length of 6 inches and a width of about 3/5 inch. Around Florida, in the Gulf of Mexico and the Caribbean Sea, *Cestum veneris* is the corresponding ctenophore; often delicate violet in color, it sometimes grows to 4-1/2 feet long.

The thimble-shaped comb-jellies lack tentacles and have a widely open gullet leading to the digestive cavity. *Beroë cucumis* is cosmopolitan but stays where the water is cool; its pinkish body is usually between 1-1/4 and 3-1/2 inches long but may be as much as 8 inches. A sea thimble at the surface south of Chesapeake Bay is more likely to be *B. ovata*, of smaller size and greater transparency.

The strangest comb-jellies are those that have comb plates only during the larval stage. *Tjalfiella* develops in this way and associates with sea pens in the icy waters along the coast of western Greenland. It was recognized to be a ctenophore only because it carries its characteristic young in a brood pouch on its back until they are ready to transform to the adult form. Members of the genus *Gastrodes* are unusual in living as internal parasites of free-swimming tunicates *(Salpa)*. As more is learned about the ghostly members of this little phylum, their roles in the economy of the sea will become better appreciated. Certainly they transform minute animals into larger pieces that a fish might eat. Some comb-jellies, in fact, are now suspected of transmitting tapeworm infections.

The Flatworms *(Phylum Platyhelminthes)*

The lowliest of worms are almost all so ribbon-thin that their popular name, which is a literal translation of "Platyhelminthes," is especially appropriate. The characteristic flatness gives them an upper and a lower surface. An anterior end is identified by behavior and by the arrangement of the simple nervous system, which coordinates the many reactions. Together these features confer a bilateral symmetry, which is much more like that in our own bodies than is to be found in any modification of the radial pattern seen in comb-jellies, cnidarians, and some sponges. Yet flatworms that possess a digestive cavity have only a blind, branched sac; the mouth serves both for eating and discharging undigested wastes.

Within the cellular layer that surrounds whatever digestive, reproductive and nervous system the flatworm has between its upper and lower surfaces, distinct muscle bands crisscross and contract in ways that allow the creature to turn right or left, swim in sinuous waves that progress from front to rear, twist its body in turning over, or wrap it against a support. Most flatworms carry out these activities in such secluded places that they are rarely seen. Yet the are far more numerous and widespread than is generally appreciated.

More than three-fourths of all the known kinds of flatworms are parasitic on or in other animals. Flukes outnumber all the rest and are grouped in the Class Trematoda. They have a mouth and digest food inside their one-piece body. The fluke lacks an epidermis, but is covered by a cuticle, and holds to its host by at least one sucker. Tapeworms, which constitute the Class Cestoda, lack a mouth as well as an epidermis. Usually they have at least two subdivisions to the body. The anterior subdivision (the scolex) has a relatively long life and holds to the host. The remainder of the body is a product of the scolex and consists of a short or long series of reproductive units (the proglottids) which can be dropped off and replaced. The fertilized eggs develop into larvae with 6 or 10 sharp hooks.

The most versatile and least specialized flatworms possess an epidermis which, for at least part of their lives, is ciliated below the body. The beating cilia create a swirling turbulence that can be seen through a low-power microscope. From the Latin word *turbella* (turbulence) comes the name of the Class Turbellaria to which these ciliated flatworms are assigned.

The Turbellarians (Class Turbellaria)

Although some kinds of flatworms are heavily pigmented and opaque, most are so transparent that whatever inner organs they possess can be seen easily once the animal is illuminated from below. The space into which the mouth opens is the feature that scientists have chosen in classifying the turbellarians. Those of Order Acoela have the mouth and pharynx leading only to an internal mass of nutritive cells. In Order Rhabdocoela it opens into an unbranched or slightly branched straight cavity. In Order Tricladida, the cavity is 3-branched, with one extension anteriorly and two posteriorly from the middle of the body where the mouth opens through a muscular pharynx. In Order Polycladida, the digestive cavity is multibranched and usually quite irregular.

Acoels are exclusively marine and less than 1/5 inch long. A tiny kind *(Aphanostoma diversicolor)*, 1/12 inch in length, tapers to a point at both ends, and often contrasts with the sea lettuce, eelgrass or other plants upon which it creeps by being yellowish at the anterior end, dark reddish purple to black near the posterior end, with a white V separating the two colored areas. Common along the southern coasts of New England, it is found also on shorelines of western Europe and in the Mediterranean Sea. In North American waters it is often outnumbered by a reddish orange to orange acoel *(Polychoerus caudatus)*, 1/6 inch long, the shape of an arrowhead, with a posterior notch in which are from one to five small tail-like appendages.

Rhabdocoels find a place in many habitats along the sea coast, in brackish and fresh water, and are in such intimate association with larger animals, including sea cucumbers and pond turtles, that no one is quite sure whether the relationship is parasitic or not. Some kinds reproduce not only sexually but also asexually by elongation and transverse division. Pale threadlike chains of individuals that have not yet separated are sometimes seen traveling in tandem. If a *Catenula,* each one will have its own unbranched digestive cavity.

65

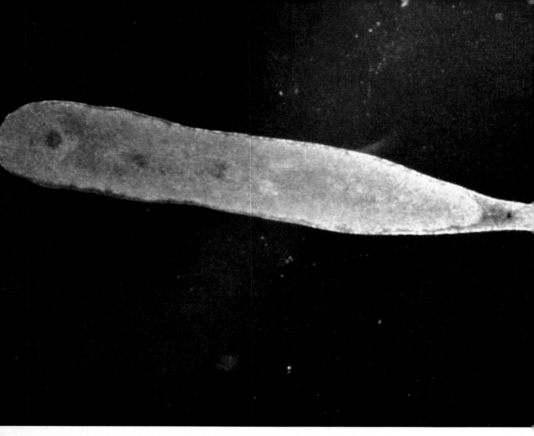

Freshwater Rhabdocoel (Stenostomum sp.)

If a *Microstomum*, the digestive cavity will have small pouches along each side. Up to 32 catenulas have been seen linked in this way, but a chain of 18 microstomums is unusually long. In marine situations, *M. davenporti* is often the only common flatworm with this habit. A freshwater member of this genus, which feeds on hydras, has the strange ability to digest all of its prey except the stinging cells, which it transfers to its own upper surface, without discharging them, and repels predators by using the very weapons of its own victims.

The most famous free-living flatworms in the world are those of the North American genus *Dugesia*, generally known as planarians. Not only do these freshwater members of Order Tricladida include the largest native freshwater turbellarian (*D. doratocephala*, 1 inch long, from spring-fed marshes) and show amazing ability to regenerate whole worms from small pieces, but they also can learn to run a maze to reach food in a psychologist's laboratory. For a while the claim was made that *Dugesia tigrina*, 4/5 inch long, could pass on its

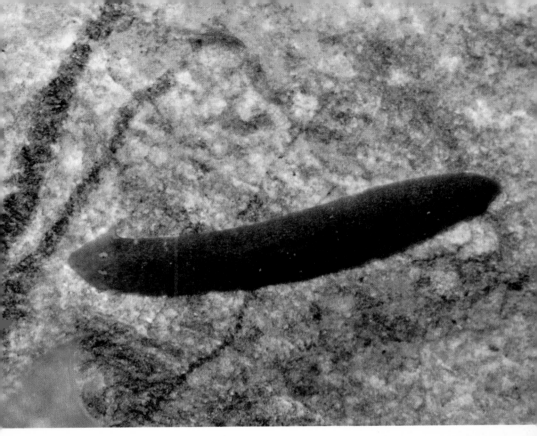

Freshwater Planarian (Dugesia sp.)

education in a maze merely by being cut into fine pieces and fed to an uneducated "naive" flatworm of the same kind. The cannibal seemingly gained molecules of memory. It learned to run the same maze correctly with far fewer trials than if its diet included only similar pieces of worms that had lived all their lives in the culture tank. Then experimenters discovered that the cannibal showed the same improved behavior if fed pieces of flatworms that had merely been handled, such as being transferred a few times each day from one culture dish to another. No one has learned yet what chemical substance forms in a worm that is handled and then stimulates another to learn faster. But at least memory of right turns and left was not transferred as was originally supposed.

Dugesia is unlike most other freshwater triclads in having a pointed anterior end and two earlike sensory lobes on either side in line with the conspicuous eyes. Each eye shows as a pale area with a jet-black spot toward the midline of the body. Shielded by the pigment of the spot are the light-sensitive cells with which the animal learns which way the light is brightest, and hence how to turn away and reach the shade. The sensory lobes probably enable the worm to direct its course toward any decaying meat in a pond or stream. A piece of bait placed under a stone will generally attract dozens of these and other flatworms in just a few hours.

Along the New England coast and around the North Atlantic to Scandinavia and Britain, a dark 1/5-inch flatworm with two eyes and a pair of diverging, forward-pointing sensory lobes is likely to be a *Procerodes*. Members of this genus that are slightly larger, pale bodied and completely eyeless live in the stream that flows through Mammoth Cave, Kentucky. Versatility in fitting different ways of life seems more conspicuous than the structural features by means of which one *Procerodes* is known from another.

A triclad flatworm with a posterior sucker below its body associates with the horseshoe crab *(Limulus)* from Maine to Cape Hatteras. Generally clinging to the shell close to the gills or on the hard plates that protect these organs, the worm *(Bdelloura candida)* twists and turns actively. If separated, it swims by undulating the thin margins of its body, which may be grayish white to yellow. Two eyes close together are near the pointed anterior end. Behind them the brown branches of the digestive tract and the white, cylindrical pharynx show through the body wall. Big individuals are fully an inch long and 1/4 inch wide.

The most spectacular triclad that can be met in North America is an introduced species *(Bipalium kewense)* that was originally discovered in a greenhouse at Kew Gardens in England. Probably it came from the Indo-Malayan rain forest. Now it can be met in greenhouses on most continents, and outdoors upon occasion in damp gardens from Florida to California. Fully expanded individuals may be 14 inches long, striped and spotted with chocolate-brown, and glide on a mucus secreted by the lower epidermis. The head end of this amazing flatworm is crescentic, with a row of minute black eyes detecting any light from the direction in which the worm is going.

Polyclads are all marine, and range in size from 6 inches down. An oval, 1-inch kind *(Stylochus ellipticus)* with a pair of short tentacles and 8 to 12 eyes on its back annoys shellfishermen by feeding on oysters as well as barnacles along the Atlantic coast from Nova Scotia to Connecticut. Farther south and around the Gulf of Mexico, similar damage is reported from *S. frontalis*, which has eyes all around its 1-inch body. Larger and smaller species of the same genus cause less comment because they prey on fouling organisms on rocks and pilings, or live in the whelk shells that large hermit crabs are carrying about.

North of Cape Cod and around the Atlantic Ocean to Scandinavia, the commonest polyclad is *Notoplana atomata* (formerly called *Leptoplana variabilis*). It lacks tentacles and wears its eyes in four conspicuous clusters some distance back from the anterior end of the narrow, 1-inch body. Its color varies from yellowish brown to pale pink, often marked with orange-brown spots. This pattern helps conceal the worm as it creeps about on wharf pilings and among the stones at the bottom of tide pools.

The Flukes (Class Trematoda)

The *trema* (hole) from which the flukes take their class name is actually the concavity of the thick-rimmed sucker on the ventral surface with which these parasites hold to their host. An additional sucker may surround the mouth, which is usually at the anterior end. It opens into a digestive tract that typically is "λ"-shaped, with many branches on each side. The food consists of body fluids or particles of tissue from the host, sucked in by muscular action of the pharynx.

Members of the Order Monogenea ("one host") are most similar to turbellarians and develop directly from a ciliated larva that swims about. It must find a host before its reserve of food is exhausted, or die. A majority of species become external parasites on fishes, amphibians, and aquatic reptiles, but some invade the mouth or urinary bladder. Sometimes the 1/8-inch *Gyrodactylus urna* infests trout and other freshwater fishes in hatcheries so heavily that they die.

All members of the Order Digenea ("two hosts") are internal parasites and show extreme adaptations in larval development as they progress from the intermediate host (or hosts) to the final ("definitive") host in which the fluke can mature, mate, and lay eggs. This may occur in its digestive tract, lungs, urinary bladder, or blood stream.

Blood flukes of the genus *Schistosoma* are devastating parasites of mankind in much of Africa, the Middle East, the Far East, South America, and parts of the West Indies. But in North America the native kinds infest only ducks and other waterfowl. The flukes mature in the blood vessels of the intestinal wall and perforate that wall to lay their fertilized eggs into the gut contents. The developing embryos pass out with the bird's wastes and hatch as ciliated larvae with a limited food supply. In less than 24 hours they must reach a freshwater snail of a suitable kind and burrow into its body. There the larva feeds and transforms into a baglike worm that reproduces asexually by internal budding.

Overleaf: left, Pacific Coast Polyclad (Allioplana californica); right, Fluke from Swordfish

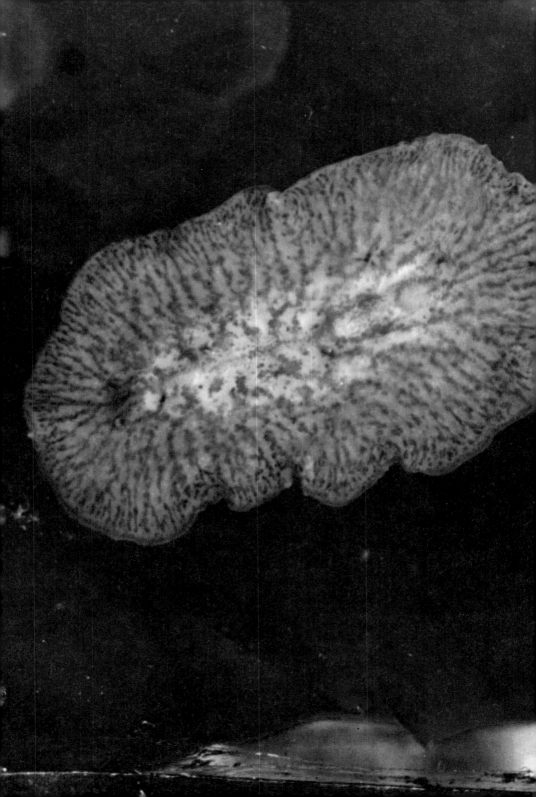

Each bud has its own small mouth, sucking pharynx, and short digestive tract. Escaping into the snail's tissues, the bud feeds and grows until it too can reproduce itself asexually. Finally, the products of all this multiplication inside the snail transform again, into free-swimming forms with a disc-shaped body and a slender, forked, propulsive tail. They emerge into the water and swim about. If they can reach the skin of the leg on a water bird or be swallowed by it, the developing worms penetrate into the blood stream. They ride to the lungs, to the liver, and finally to the veins along the intestine where they mature.

Particularly in lakes of the north-central United States and Canada, the number of the fork-tailed larvae searching for a water bird can be tremendous by midsummer. The larvae attack human swimmers and penetrate the skin, but cannot survive in human blood. The skin, however, becomes irritated and shows "swimmer's itch." Repeated exposure may produce a severe rash and even prostration as an allergic response. Bathers can minimize the effect by swimming vigorously, then leaving the water and wiping the skin dry immediately with a rough towel. Or they can maximize the annoyance by playing in shallow water, getting alternately wet and dry.

Two intermediate hosts are needed for a complete life history by many digenetic flukes. Examples can be found in the 1/30-inch flukes of the genus *Bucephalus* that commonly infest the small intestine in carnivorous fishes both in fresh waters and the seas. The fertilized eggs pass out with the wastes of the fish and hatch into ciliated larvae that search out a suitable bivalve mollusk. It may be a clam *(Anodonta,* or *Unio)* in a river or lake or an oyster along a sea coast. Entering the digestive gland of the bivalve, the larva transforms into the form that reproduces asexually. The products of this multiplication, however, are free-swimming individuals with a disc-shaped body and an unforked slender tail. They emerge into the water and swim off to find small fishes. Seizing on any they meet, they transform into dormant cysts under the scales or on the fins. In this site they wait until, by chance, the small fish is eaten by one of the carnivorous fishes. When the cyst wall has been digested away, the young fluke emerges and attaches itself to the lining of the host's intestine, where it can mature.

The Tapeworms (Class Cestoda)

As adults, all tapeworms live in the small intestine of some vertebrate animal. They rely upon the host to find, eat, and digest their food. The worms compete

Scolex of Pork Tapeworm (Taenia solium)

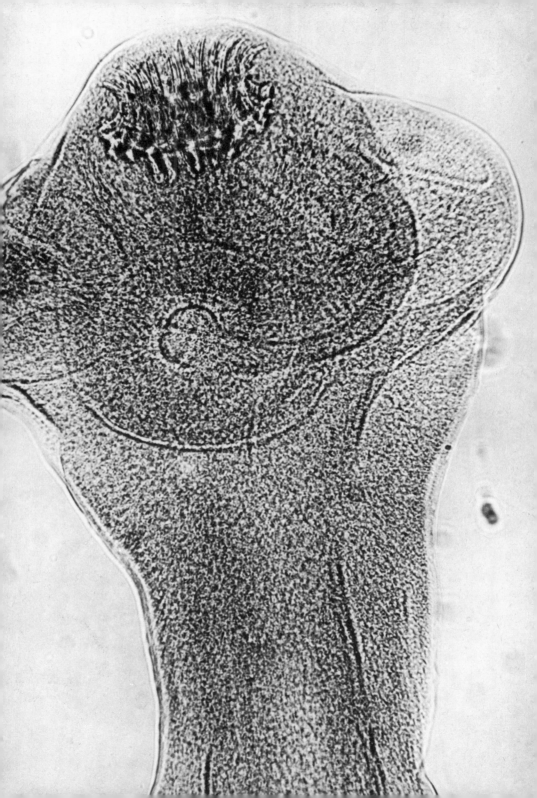

in absorbing the products of digestion through their body walls and have no need for any mouth or digestive organs of their own. The adaptations of a tapeworm resemble those of many flukes in promoting the chance that the larvae from fertilized eggs will eventually reach the intestine of a suitable host. Each tapeworm has to be eaten in order to find a suitable destination.

In North America, human dietary habits and public health regulations keep to a minimum the number of people who become infected with tapeworms. Any trend in taste toward eating rare beef or beef products that are not fully cooked improves the chance that the beef tapeworm *(Taenia saginata)* will find a new host; mature worms of this kind may be 80 feet long, with as many as 2,000 proglotids. Insufficiently cooked pork products, including cured hams, provide a source of the pork tapeworm *(Taenia solium)*. Raw or poorly cooked fish may contain live encysted stages of the fish tapeworm *(Dibothriocephalus latus)*, which often reaches a length of 60 feet with perhaps 4,000 proglottids. Dogs and cats that appear quite healthy often harbor a tapeworm *(T. pisiformis)* that goes through its larval stages in rabbits, or another *(T. taeniaeformis)* of which rats and mice are intermediate hosts, or the dog tapeworm *(Dipylidium caninum)* whose early development is in fleas and dog lice.

The commonest tapeworm in man is a dwarf *(Hymenolepis nana)* less than 2 inches long. Its eggs may be eaten by fleas or flour beetles, which then serve as intermediate hosts. Or the eggs may be swallowed and the larvae go through their developmental stages in the wall of the human intestine if food is contaminated with particles of human feces.

So widespread are these particular parasites in domestic animals and humans today that parasitologists can only guess where the specific tapeworms originated. Those of the dog, cat, pig, and cow probably adopted their hosts long before man domesticated them. Through his enterprise they became virtually cosmopolitan.

The fish tapeworm can develop to maturity in man just as well in a bear, a fox, a raccoon or other fish-eating mammal. Its eggs can continue development only if they reach fresh water. There they hatch into ciliated larvae that enter small crustaceans, such as the common copepod *Cyclops*. Developing one step in the body cavity of the crustacean, the larva waits until this intermediate host is swallowed by a fish such as a perch, trout, or pike. Burrowing into the fish, the larval tapeworm grows as much as 4/5 inch long and becomes dormant in muscle tissues. There it waits again until swallowed by the final host.

All of the larger tapeworms accommodate their extraordinary length to the space available in the small intestine of the final host. This portion of the digestive tract is ordinarily well filled with fluid, including the food upon which enzymes are working. The tapeworm loops itself back and forth and swims continually to keep the long string of its maturing proglottids well spaced. Only as the terminal proglottids break away, each filled with developing embryos, do they cease activity and let themselves be carried to the outside world.

The Ribbon Worms *(Phylum Nemertea)*

To the beachcomber who, for the first time, finds a ribbon worm, it appears to be a flatworm or a roundworm of some kind. It is clearly not segmented. In size, it may be anywhere between a fraction of an inch and 20 feet long and in color, a plain brownish-black, tan, yellow, green, orange, red, purple, or white. Some are patterned with contrasting crossbands or longitudinal stripes. Colored markings may make the head seem distinct, but a slight expansion and several (or many) eyes are the only other features likely to help distinguish the front end from the more pointed rear.

Some of the small ribbon worms will attempt to defend themselves by shooting out a long, tubular proboscis from a muscular sheath that lies above the digestive tract. The proboscis serves also to capture prey, to attach the worm to solid objects as it creeps about, and to burrow in sand or mud. In several of the commonest ribbon worms the proboscis tip is armed with a sharp spike or stylet, which the animal drives into its prey so accurately on the first try that the Greek word for "unerring" was used as the basis for the phylum name.

Like a flatworm, a ribbon worm has a cellular mesenchyme filling all the spaces between its inner organs. But the digestive tract is a straight tube leading from mouth to anus and is lined with ciliated cells rather like those that form the epidermis over the soft body. The eversible proboscis is unique and completely separate from the digestive tube. The bilateral symmetry is shown also in the nervous system, which consists of a small ganglion just above and in front of (or behind) the mouth, plus two lengthwise lateral nerves and sometimes a mid-dorsal nerve trunk. Blood, which may be red or colorless, circulates forward and back in three lengthwise blood vessels with contractile walls, and also through cross connections in the anterior end and around the digestive tract.

About 50 kinds of ribbon worms live along the Atlantic coast of North America, 20 near the Gulf coast, and 100 along the Pacific. Half a dozen species

Overleaf: left, Primitive Ribbon Worm (Tubulanus polymorphus);
right, Cylindrical Ribbon Worm (Lineus pictifrons)

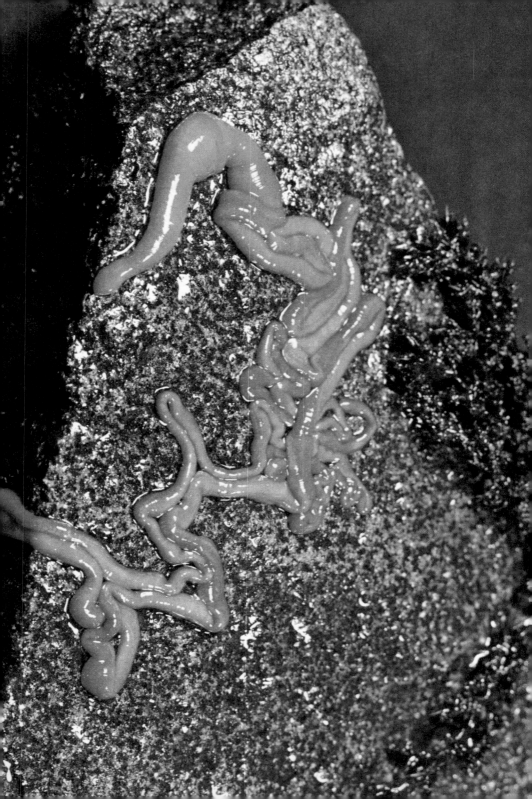

are common to all three regions. The species *Prostomum rubrum* represents the sole genus found in freshwater pools and quiet streams in most parts of the United States and southern Canada. A reddish worm less than 1 inch long, it clings to aquatic plants where it finds minute crustaceans, turbellarians, and roundworms to eat. The only genus of terrestrial nemerteans *(Geonemertes)* has one of its two species in Bermuda, but none on the North American continent.

All except two of these ribbon worms in the United States and Canada seem to be free-living predators, even though they may occasionally cluster together in social groups. One of the exceptions is *Malacobdella grossa*, less than 2 inches long. It is a yellowish white worm with star-shaped spots and a posterior sucker. It lives as a harmless guest in the mantle cavity of various clams. The other, *Carcinonemertes carcinophila*, is a parasite on various kinds of crabs. A mated pair of these slender worms, which are red with a single pair of black eyes at the anterior end, is often found within a thick sheath of mucus that they have secreted on the crab's gills or among its egg masses.

One of the widely distributed nemerteans is *Tubulanus pellucidus*, with a slender white body as much as an inch long, found in delicate transparent tubes among seaweeds from the intertidal zone to a depth of at least 60 feet. Although the head is broad, the worm lacks eyes, as do all the members of the primitive Order Paleonemertea to which it belongs.

Ranging only from the Bay of Fundy to the Texas coast is an equally slender, cylindrical nemertean *(Lineus socialis)* that may be 6 inches long and olive-green to reddish brown marked with white on the sides of the head. When disturbed it often coils into a spiral. Under stones and among mussels in the intertidal zone it slithers along extended to full length. It can reproduce asexually by fragmentation as well as sexually, and shows such incredible powers of regeneration that scientists have studied it intensively. When cut into small pieces, each fragment that contains a portion of one nerve cord will reorganize itself into a minute replica of the original worm.

The longest of North American ribbon worms are members of the genus *Cerebratulus*, which burrow in intertidal muds and sands. They can replace the posterior end of the body if it is broken off, but not the triangular head with its lengthwise slit of a mouth and its terminal pore through which the proboscis is extended. Yet so long as the temperature is low and the sea water is renewed periodically, worms of this kind can fast for a year or more while gradually shrinking in size. Throughout this ordeal the animals remain alert, normal in appearance, and keep their adult color, which may be pink, yellow, or white.

Young cerebratulids tend to be translucent white and show their brown paired pouches along the intestine through the thin body wall.

The Aschelminths *(Phylum Aschelminthes)*

Some of the world's most inconspicuous animals and many of its commonest and most widespread kinds have been grouped together in this phylum. All of them are essentially wormlike with a complete digestive tube but no circulatory or respiratory organs and no well-formed head. Their most unifying feature is the body cavity within which their organs lie free. It corresponds to the space produced during embryonic development when the dividing cells of the fertilized egg rearrange themselves slightly to form a hollow ball. The hollow in most kinds of animals becomes filled and obliterated. In the aschelminths it remains as the body cavity and is occupied by a fluid that serves some of the functions of blood.

Mermithid Roundworm parasite emerging from a Wolf Spider

The commonest and most widespread members of this phylum are the round-worms (Class Nematoda) and the microscopic wheel animalcules (Class Rotifera). The minor groups are the kinorhynchs (Class Kinorhyncha or Echinodera), the gastrotrichs (Class Gastrotricha), and the horsehair worms (Class Nemato-morpha or Gordiacea). Two other groups have a body cavity of almost identical origin, but are excluded from the Aschelminthes because of impressive differences in other respects: the parasitic, spiny-headed worms (Phylum Acanthocephala) and the tiny entoprocts (Phylum Entoprocta or Kamptozoa). These groups probably evolved together from some ancestral type of turbellarian flatworm, but gave rise to no other classes or phyla.

The Roundworms (Class Nematoda or Nemathelminthes)

Writing of roundworms in the *Yearbook* of the United States Department of Agriculture, a scientist who had studied them intensively claimed that

If all the matter in the universe except the nematodes were swept away, our world would still be dimly recognizable, and if, as disembodied spirits, we could then investigate it, we should find its mountains, hills, vales, rivers, lakes and oceans represented by a thin film of nematodes. The location of towns would be decipherable, since for every massing of human beings there would be a corresponding massing of certain nematodes. Trees would still stand in ghostly rows representing our streets and high-ways. The location of the various plants and animals would still be deci-pherable, and, had we sufficient knowledge, in many cases even their species could be determined by an examination of their erstwhile nematode parasites.

With only about 10,000 species recognized so far and many of them predators and scavengers, the identification of host plants and animals would rest partly on combinations of roundworms afflicting each and partly on recognizing the many still unnamed species. For man this pattern would vary somewhat on a geographical basis, with the hookworm *Necator americanus* in the United States and a different one in the Old World, with the trichina worm *(Trichinella spiralis)* in areas where pork products and bear meat are eaten insufficiently cooked, with the pinworm (or seatworm, *Enterobius vermicularis)* virtually cosmopolitan, but exotics such as the dreaded guinea worm *(Dracunculus medinensis)* and filarias (especially *Wuchereria bancrofti)* among travelers who have been exposed to infection in Africa and Asia.

Free-living nematodes are often abundant in the bottom mud along sea coasts, in marshes and swamps, lakes and streams, and in the soil. A few live in hot springs, on glaciers, and in the water that collects among the leaf bases of epiphytic plants in tropical rain forests. Probably the terrestrial species had marine ancestors, and provided the colonists that spread into freshwater habitats. Many of the terrestrial and freshwater roundworms are cosmopolitan, perhaps distributed by insects and migrating birds. The minute eggs of nematodes that live among clumps of moss and lichens are especially tolerant of extreme and prolonged desiccation, and almost certainly are dispersed as dust by wind.

In the soil, roundworms remain where they have a film of moisture to slide through around the mineral particles. After a rain great numbers of nematodes come to the surface and feed on organic matter or on smaller animals that are present. A single rotting apple on the ground below an apple tree has been found to contain 90,000 roundworms of several different species taking advantage of the opportunities. Samples of good farm soil contain so many nematodes that the population has been calculated to range between several hundred thousand and many billions to the acre. That these estimates are realistic is confirmed by scientists who count as many as 4,420,000 roundworms per square meter in the bottom mud along the sea coast.

The truly amazing aspect of the roundworms is that they have been able to evolve so many different ways of life with so little modification of their body structure. All of these animals are long, cylindrical, totally devoid of appendages or even cilia. A heavy cuticle covers their slim bodies. It is the elastic and multi-layered product of an epidermis that forms parallel longitudinal cords from mouth to anus and may not be divided into cells but have nuclei in rows. Lengthwise muscle bands alternate with these cords and are bathed on the inner surface by the fluid in the body cavity. No circulatory mechanism is needed. The wriggling of the worm churns the fluid and distributes the food materials that have been absorbed into it from the central digestive tract.

The habitat and food habits of a roundworm can often be guessed from an examination of its mouth region. A marine nematode is likely to possess from 6 to 10 liplike lobes, whereas a terrestrial (or freshwater or parasitic) nematode ordinarily has only three, one of which is dorsal. Plain lips, such as are seen in the 1/2-inch vinegar eels *(Anguillula aceti)*, that are often common (and harmless) among the cloud of fungus particles at the bottom of a bottle of old vinegar, go with soft foods in microscopic units. Elaborate crowns of teeth on the lips generally indicate a carnivorous or parasitic habit. Some carnivorous roundworms and many that feed on the contents of plant cells have a long solid or hollow spear that can be protruded from the mouth. The hollow spear serves both to puncture the source of food and as a tube through which the fluid contents can be pumped out by muscular action of the worm's pharynx. No roundworm chews its food.

The hooks of a hookworm are teeth on its lips. They are used as anchors and as piercing structures. With them the 1/2-inch adult hookworm lacerates the cells lining the small intestine of its host and induces hemorrhage. Then the worm sucks in a mixture of blood, lymph, cell debris, and contents of the host's gut. If many hookworms are active in the same intestine, they cause much loss of blood and make the host anemic. Without letting go or ceasing to feed, the adult female hookworms drop several thousand eggs daily into the gut contents, and these pass out in the feces. If left in a moist, shady, warm place the eggs hatch in two to four days, and the larvae feed on whatever organic matter is available to them in the feces or on the soil surface. Then, at a length of about 1/50 inch, they become infective for man. They gain entry by burrowing through the soft skin on the sides of the foot or elsewhere when people walk about barefooted or kneel or lie on infected soil. Penetration causes "ground itch." Entering the lymph stream or the blood vessels, the larvae eventually reach the lungs, where they break through into the air passages. Traveling up the windpipe, they reach the gullet and are carried down to the intestine, where they may live for months or even years. Transmission of these parasites is blocked by sanitary disposal of feces and the wearing of shoes.

The human pinworm shows even simpler adaptations to parasitic life. This cosmopolitan species infects almost every child and sometimes university students who help support themselves by baby-tending. New hosts get infected by ingesting particles of dirt containing the eggs of the worm. These are not only in feces but also scattered inconspicuously on the bedding, clothes, hands and abundantly under the fingernails of an infected child. The eggs are picked up and dispersed when the child scratches the region around its anus. There, during the night, female pinworms deposit eggs and cause intense itching before retreating into the rectum. Since the ingested eggs hatch quickly and the worms grow as they move down to the large intestine as the site for maturation and mating, infections are spread easily. A child is likely to continually reinfect itself.

Two hosts are commonly, but not necessarily, involved in the life history of the gapeworm *(Syngamus trachea)* of domestic fowl. This parasite tends to cluster with others of its kind in the bird's windpipe, causing the host to gasp for breath and cough. Coughing frees some of the adult gapeworms, which are then swallowed. The host may digest them, but not their eggs, which pass out with the feces. On the soil, the developing eggs are commonly swallowed by earthworms but not digested. If a fowl eats a contaminated earthworm (or food that is fouled with feces and gapeworm eggs), the nematode larvae hatch out in the bird's intestine. Parasitologists suspect that the gapeworm larvae follow the same route as hookworms in reaching the windpipe, where they grow to maturity.

Often the eggs of roundworms are easier to find in fecal samples than any other identifiable symptom of the parasites' presence. The tough waterproof covering of the egg may show features in size, shape, and surface markings that allow a skilled parasitologist to recognize the infection without seeing the worm at all. Generally, the recommended treatment for the host is a drug accompanied by a laxative or purge. The drug causes the worms to release their hold long enough to be swept out with the feces.

For the minute or microscopic roundworms that attack the roots of plants and cause crop losses, quite different treatments are necessary. Once an infection has begun, it can seldom be halted because the root tissue of the plant proliferates around the worm or worms, forming a gall that effectively shields the parasite. Where the nematode restricts itself to a single kind of plant or a few closely related kinds, as *Heterodera schachtii* does with sugar beets and other beets, the farmer can put in different crops for several years until the soil has freed itself of this infection. But for root parasites that spread to crop plants from native trees and weeds, the agriculturalist must either rely upon drenching the soil with selective pesticides (and risk destroying many other forms of life as well) or upon special genetic strains of the crop that plant breeders develop for resistance to root nematodes.

Only a specialist can reliably identify either the parasitic or the free-living nematodes. The primary subdivision of the phylum into classes is based largely on the peculiar sense organs found at the anterior and posterior ends. In Class Phasmidea (or Secernentea), a pair of posterolateral organs ("phasmids") are usually present, but the anterolateral organs ("amphids") are mere pores. This combination is found in the sugar-beet nematode, the hookworms and filaria worms as well as many free-living roundworms in soil, fresh and salt waters. In Class Aphasmidia (or Adenophorea), the posterolateral sense organs are lacking, and the anterolateral pair have various forms other than porelike. This class includes the trichina worm and the particularly widespread enoplids (such as *Enoplus* and *Trilobus*), found in salt, brackish and fresh waters and in soil. Apparently each species, however, has a narrow tolerance for salinity, for no nematodes are known from both salt and fresh water.

The Kinorhynchs (Class Kinorhyncha or Echinodera)

The 30 different kinds of tiny worms that constitute this peculiar group are all less than 1/25 inch long. They resemble roundworms only in a complete lack of cilia, a thick cuticle, a straight digestive tract, and the type of body cavity. Each kinorhynch, however, keeps its cuticle folded into 13 or 14 overlapping rings that match a repetitive pattern in its musculature and nervous system. Most kinds have a pair of minute eyes behind the retractile proboscis that bears the mouth. Hooks and spines arm the proboscis, while spines and bristles project from many of the cuticular rings on the rest of the body, both at the sides and above. At the posterior end, these animals bear two or four particularly stout bristles that often suggest a forked tail.

Kinorhynchs pull themselves along by means of the armament on the proboscis, which accounts for their class names. Kinorhynch is literally "locomotory beak" and echinodere is "spiny skin." Found only in marine situations, the kinorhynchs burrow in the superficial sand and mud close to shore and at considerable depths. They live also in the slimy covering on mollusks and crabs. Probably in both places they find microscopic algal cells and organic debris to suck in and digest.

Although kinorhynchs have been discovered in places as widely separated as Antarctica, Zanzibar, and Japan, fewer than a dozen kinds are known from North America. Two bristles terminate the body and only the first head ring is retractile in *Echinoderella*, of which *E. steineri* has been collected in Texas and *E. remanei* in Maine. Four tail bristles and two retractile head rings are characteristic of the other two species from Maine: *Pycnophyes frequens* and *Trachydemus mainensis*.

The Gastrotrichs (Class Gastrotricha)

A microscope is needed to find a gastrotrich, for all 170 different species mature at minute dimensions, between 1/400 and 1/20 inch in length. They can be mistaken easily for protozoans as they creep about among the bottom ooze in fresh and salt water. But each one has a complete digestive tract, delicate bands of lengthwise muscles, and an epidermis that secretes a heavy cuticle. Arising from the cuticle are many bristles and spines, or the surface may be marked off into a mosaic pattern of firm plates or scales that overlap like shingles. The under surface bears cilia that serve in locomotion. Each individual possesses both ovaries and testes, but among the members of the one order that has representatives in both freshwater and marine habitats, the male function is ordinarily suppressed and reproduction is by virgin birth (parthenogenesis).

About 60 per cent of the gastrotrichs known are freshwater representatives of the Chaetonotoidea. The generic names of the commonest genera describe the appearance of these animals: *Chaetonotus* ("bristly back") and *Lepidodermella* ("little scaly skin"). Members of *Neodasys* are marine. Characteristically in this order, the head region is set off from the rest of the body by a necklike narrowing, and the little worms hold on by means of adhesive tubes at the posterior end only. Members of the order Macrodasyoidea are exclusively marine. They have a more linear body, with adhesive tubes located at both ends and along the sides as though anchorage were more of a challenge in their way of life. Among sand particles and detritus along sea coasts, the species of *Macrodasys* and *Urodasys* are often numerous. Apparently all gastrotrichs feed on unicellular algae and minute particles of organic matter that they can suck into their digestive tubes.

The Wheel Animalcules (Class Rotifera)

Virtually any sample of stagnant fresh water taken from the bottom of a ditch, an eavestrough or a bird bath abounds with free-living rotifers. Many live along the edges of ponds, marshes, and streams. A few inhabit the sea. Most of these animals are less than 1/25 inch long. But they move about so actively, investigating their watery world, that they charm any amateur microscopist. The scientist is challenged to comprehend multicellular organisms in such small sizes. They are no bigger than the larger one-celled animals, which suggests that the opportunities and hazards they meet must be comparable.

The class is named for a "rotation" or "wheel" effect that is an illusion produced by the beating cilia that generally form a ring or two at the anterior end. These are the only cilia the animal possesses, and serve to create a water current. This the rotifer can use to propel itself, or to bring it particles of food, such as bacteria and unicellular algae. Once through the mouth and the short pharynx, the food particles enter a grinding organ in which hard teeth hold, chop and grind the food. The remainder of the alimentary tract is a fair-sized stomach with digestive glands and a short intestine, which opens at the base of a forked locomotory appendage called the foot. It may be divided into two or four "toes," each with a cement gland that the rotifer uses to attach itself temporarily to firm objects in its world.

Only about 50 of the approximately 1,500 different kinds of rotifers are strictly marine, and most of these are coastal. But in salt water there are other species that possess great tolerance for changes in salinity; these species are found in fresh waters too. The freshwater rotifers are largely cosmopolitan, seemingly because in autumn or under adverse conditions they produce "winter eggs" that winds and birds can disperse easily. Winter eggs have thick shells and can withstand both desiccation and extreme temperatures.

Most rotifers possess two lateral antennae and belong to the order Monogonta. They include roving types, such as turtle-shaped *Testudinella* and pear-shaped *Synchaeta;* and sedentary kinds, such as *Floscularia*, in a vaselike tube constructed from minute sand grains, or *Colletheca*, in a cylindrical mass of gelatinous secretion; or pelagic, solitary *Polyarthra*, with elongated paddlelike bristles used in jerky locomotion; or pelagic, colonial *Conochilus*, of which the individuals radiate like trumpets from a common center. One genus, *Proales*, consists of parasitic species, two of which live inside the spherical colonies of the flagellate *Volvox*. One causes galls on the filamentous alga *Vaucheria*. Another takes nourishment from polyps of *Gonothyrea*, fastening itself by the mouth to the epidermis of its host inside the protective sheath.

Members of the order Bdelloidea mainly live in clumps of mosses and shrubby lichens, where they creep about like leeches or swim when the plants are wet. Sometimes a handful of moss that has been dry in a closed jar for years will release dozens of rotifers after being rewetted for 10 to 15 minutes. The wheel animalcules that emerge are likely to be females of *Adineta*, *Embata*, *Habrotrocha*, *Philodina*, or *Rotaria*.

One additional small order, the Seisonacea, consists only of the members of genus *Seison*. They are found only under the carapace, around the gills, of certain 1/2-inch marine crustaceans *(Nebalia)* that frequent coastal waters.

The Horsehair Worms (Class Nematomorpha or Gordiacea)

Folklore holds that when a hair from a horse's tail falls or blows into a puddle, a rain barrel or a clear spring, only a few days are needed for the hair to transform into a living horsehair worm. If the water is examined carefully, a drowned beetle or cricket or grasshopper can usually be found. Some observers have been on hand to see the extremely slender black or dark brown worm emerge from the insect as it struggled to save its life.

Sometimes a tangled group of horsehair worms can be found writhing together in such places. The males mate with the females, which are longer, and these lay fertilized eggs in long gelatinous strings. The larvae that hatch out might be mistaken for kinorhynchs, because they are covered by a cuticle that is folded into about 20 telescoping rings. But the larvae manage to enter a large arthropod. In its body they grow as internal parasites, absorbing most of their nourishment through their body wall and scarcely using their degenerate digestive tracts.

Various species of *Paragordius* and *Gordius*, some 12 inches long at maturity and characteristically dark colored, are common in terrestrial insects and shallow fresh water. As adults these worms have loose cells as a mesenchyme filling the body cavity. By contrast, in members of the marine genus *Nectonema*, which may become 4 inches long, the pale body retains a body cavity resembling that of a roundworm. Nectonemas sometimes swim by means of rows of special bristles protruding from the cuticle, and come at night to coastal waters that are illuminated by artificial light. Their larvae parasitize various decapod crustaceans, such as crabs and hermit crabs.

The Spiny-headed Worms
(Phylum Acanthocephala)

The burrlike "head" of a spiny-headed worm is actually a proboscis that can be retracted into a sheath at the anterior end of the cylindrical body. The animal has no mouth, nor any digestive tract. It lives as an intestinal parasite, much the way a tapeworm does, letting its host provide both the food and the digestive enzymes to make the nourishment absorbable. Ordinarily the life history includes two different hosts, the larval stage being spent in an arthropod, such as a crustacean or an insect, and the adult stage in a vertebrate that eats the infected invertebrate.

Like members of the phylum Aschelminthes, a spiny-headed worm is covered by a cuticle and has no lining of peritoneum around its body cavity. The cuticle bears the recurved hooks on the proboscis, and often spines on the trunk region where it may be folded into telescoping rings that indicate no segmentation but provide flexibility. Under the cuticle is a fibrous epidermis, with scattered large nuclei that are not separated by cell membranes, and with peculiar canals that open neither externally nor internally. The canals are suspected of helping to distribute food as it is being absorbed. Reproductive organs, either male or female, occupy much of the space inside the body.

The fertilized eggs develop for a while inside the female before being released to pass out with the feces. Larvae hatch only after the eggs are eaten by the intermediate host. The common spiny-headed worm of the pig *(Macracanthorhynchus hirudinaceus)*, which matures at 2 to 4 inches long and 1/5 inch in diameter if a male and 4 to 13 inches long and 2/5 inch in diameter if a female, spends its larval life in the larvae of scarabaeid beetles. The 12-inch *Moniliformis dubius* of the rat has its larval development in cockroaches or beetles that inhabit houses. Occasionally the intermediate hosts are eaten by people, who then may harbor adult spiny-headed worms.

Scientists regard the 500 different kinds of acanthocephalans as constituting a separate phylum, rather than a class in Aschelminthes, because of detailed differences in the embryonic origin of the body cavity and because the body wall of the adult possesses not only longitudinal muscles (which aschelminths have) but also a sheath of encircling muscle fibers between the longitudinals and the epidermis. No aschelminth has this extra sheath of muscles, which adds greatly to the mobility of the spiny-headed worm.

The Entoprocts

(Phylum Entoprocta or Kamptozoa)

Resembling moss animals (bryozoans) or minute hydroids (hydrozoan cnidarians), the 75 different kinds of entoprocts exhibit a combination of body features that makes their relationships obscure. The individuals, which are always less than 1/5 inch tall, may be solitary or joined in colonies formed by budding. A short stalk supports the bell- or boat-shaped body, which bears a ring of 8 to 30 tentacles as extensions of the body wall. Cilia extend through the cuticle on the tentacles and create water currents that bring bacteria, algal cells and other organic particles as food. These particles are captured by the

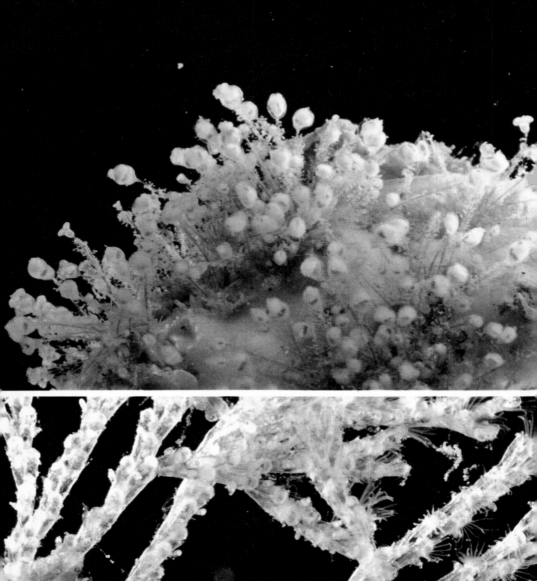

mouth and conveyed by cilia through a U-shaped digestive tract, which opens at an anus on a projection within the ring of tentacles. The phylum name, Entoprocta, indicates "inner anus," drawing attention to a difference between entoprocts and moss animals (often called ectoprocts), which have the anus outside the ring of tentacles. Unlike moss animals, which have a peritoneum lining a capacious body cavity, the entoprocts lack a peritoneum and the space between gut and epidermis is filled with a gelatinous mass containing both free and fixed cells.

The solitary entoprocts, which constitute Family Loxosomatidae, are all marine and live attached by a simple adhesive disc to sponges, tunicates, crustaceans and other sea animals or their tubes. *Loxosoma* on the Atlantic coast and *Loxocalyx* on the Pacific reproduce both sexually, with a swimming larval stage, and by budding off new individuals in a way that resembles the reproduction in hydras.

Of the colonial entoprocts, the members of just one genus *(Urnatella)* in a family of its own (Urnatellidae) live in fresh water, usually on the undersides of stones in streams of the eastern and central United States and adjacent Canada. The other genera, in the family Pedicellinidae, are all marine and widespread in shallow water. Species of *Pedicellina*, which are common on wharf pilings, have cup-shaped bodies on short, stout stalks, whereas those of *Barentsia* are more fragile in appearance, with long, slender stalks supporting almost globular bodies. When the stalks are extended, the *Barentsia* "heads" often rise 1/2 inch above the bivalve shell, or stone, or other support over which the interconnecting stolons branch. *B. laxa* is particularly common, forming furry patches, on shells of the quahog clam that have been roughened by the boring sponge *Cliona*. *B. major* attaches is little colonies aroung the bases of the legs on horseshoe crabs *(Limulus)* and spider crabs *(Libinia)*.

The Phoronids *(Phylum Phoronida)*

All 18 different members of this strange little phylum are marine and commonly inhabit vertical blind tubes in sandy ocean floors. From their upper (head) end, they extend ciliated tentacles from a crown shaped like a double horseshoe. Mucus on the tentacles captures microscopic particles of food from the water, which are then digested in a U-shaped gut with an anus just below the crown.

Entoproct colony (Barentsia)
Moss Animal colony (Bugula)

Phoronids have red blood in a closed circulatory system. Most are hermaphroditic and release fertilized eggs that develop into swimming larvae.

A few species are known from American coasts. The giant is *Phoronopsis californica*, 8 inches long but a mere 5/16 inch in diameter. Its orange body remains hidden while its bright orange tentacles extend 3/4 inch above the sand in estuaries of California. The smaller *Phoronis architecta* of North Carolina, and as far north as Chesapeake Bay, is more common and only 5 inches long and flesh-colored. Both phoronids lead solitary lives and hide from view when the tide is low.

The Moss Animals

(Phylum Bryozoa or Ectoprocta)

Moss animals are not easy to find and, since few of them are more than 1/64 inch long, a magnifying lens is helpful in observing them. They form colonies, however, that are bigger and more distinctive in appearance. Most are marine; less than 50 of the 3,500 kinds of moss animals live in fresh water.

Many marine species provide fuzzy pastel-colored growths on wharf pilings below the level that is exposed at low tide. Other bryozoans add a rough covering over a snail shell, or coat the rocky walls of a tide pool that waves scour at least twice each day. Still others encrust blades of seaweed with a limy coating known as "lace coral." Many attach themselves to boat hulls as members of the unappreciated community of "fouling organisms" that must be scraped off periodically.

Each individual bryozoan lives for a few weeks attached to the walls of a chamber formed of its own secretion. It extends tentacles in a group that may be circular, oval, or horseshoe-shaped. The tentacles differ from those of coelenterates in bearing cilia. The cilia create a current of water that brings to the bryozoan bacteria and other minute particles of food. They enter its mouth, placed centrally in the group of tentacles, and continue through a U-shaped digestive tract. The anus is outside the tentacle array and thereby earns the animal its alternative name of ectoproct meaning, "outside anus." Otherwise, the body is astonishingly simple, for it contains no respiratory, circulatory, or excretory organs.

Within its chamber, a moss animal has no room for growth. It can use its peculiar system for extending and retracting its crown of tentacles only if its body fills most of its enclosure, while retaining a space into which the tentacles can be withdrawn. The tentacles are extended by a sudden increase in the hydraulic pressure of fluid in the body cavity, which occurs when certain muscles contract. Other muscles pull the everted crown back to safety at the slightest disturbance.

Through the chamber walls, interconnecting strands keep adjacent individuals in intimate contact. Around the periphery of an encrusting colony, or at the tips of the branches on those that have a shrubby form, the strands produce buds asexually. Each bud is able to enlarge as a new individual and secrete its own chamber walls. These bud parts of the colony are always the youngest. A hand lens focused back of the edges of the tips usually reveals chambers that are empty except for minute "brown bodies." A brown body is the remains of an individual that has reproduced sexually. It erupts and releases microscopic embryos that swim through the water and dies in the process of giving birth. Still older parts of the colony are likely to be reinhabited by feeding individuals, because the interconnecting strands produce buds in the chambers of the dead and provide replacements. Often the first meal of the replacing individual is the brown body representing its predecessor.

Differences in the form and arrangement of the chambers in bryozoan colonies provide useful clues for identifying the various kinds. Those of order Cyclostomata secrete a simple limy tube, open at the end from which the crown of tentacles is extended. The contraction of muscles around the opening of the chamber compresses the fluid in the body cavity and ejects the tentacle crown; retraction is at the expense of space in the chamber opening through which the feeding organ is withdrawn. This kind of moss animal has been in existence at least since Upper Cambrian times more than 500 million years ago and is represented in coastal communities today by shrubby little *Crisia* and creeping or erect colonies of *Tubulipora*.

A comblike array of spines and bristles provides some protection over the retracted tentacles in members of order Ctenostomata (the "comb mouths"), whose ancestry dates back to Ordovician days. These moss animals produce a chitinous or gelatinous tube without lime. They are represented on pilings, seaweeds, and immersed rocks along the sea coast by the widespread vase-clustered *Bowerbankia gracilis*, which grows from a creeping "stolon," and by *Flustrellidra hispida*, which forms brown rubbery crusts on kelps and even the thin fronds of sea lettuce. In brackish water, *Victorella pavida* often forms

Overleaf: left, Sea Lace colony (Membranipora electra); right, Freshwater Moss Animal colony (Plumatella sp.)

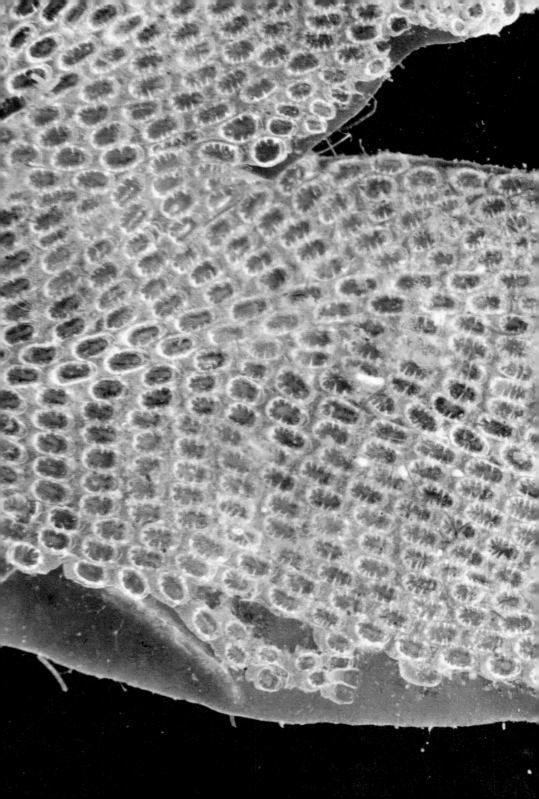

plushlike mats 1/2 inch thick, varying in color according to the nature of the earthy material that has been incorporated into the chamber walls as supplementary stiffening. In fresh waters all over the world, the related *Paludicella ehrenbergii* often has a vinelike appearance, partly creeping and partly erect on sticks and stones in slow streams and permanent ponds.

Most modern moss animals belong to the marine order Cheilostomata, in which the chamber of each individual bears a movable lip, like a hinged door. In some members of this order, the doors extend as long, whiplike organs that can be swept over the surface of the colony to keep it clean. In other members, special small non-feeding individuals develop, each resembling the highly motile head of a bird; they are called avicularia, from the Latin *avicula*, meaning a little bird. Each avicularium uses its modified door like a bird's beak to seize and hold small invaders of the colony until they die and decompose. This order includes the "lace corals" of genus *Membranipora*, which form calcareous encrustations on stones, shells and seaweeds, and also the erect, flexible, branching, treelike species of *Bugula*, in which the avicularia are especially active and efficient.

The most astonishing moss animals are those that have recently evolved in fresh waters, resisting both desiccation and winter ice. They are carried from one isolated pond or stream to another embedded in mud on the feet of water birds. The resistant stage that can travel in this way is called a statoblast; it is formed by internal budding within the colony late in summer and released when the colony dies. This is the habit of the branching *Fredericella sultana* and of the various species of *Plumatella*, which grow best in the shade or darkness and sometimes clog waterways or water pipes. It is characteristic too of the oval, gelatinous colonies of *Cristatella* that often cling to the lower surface of lily pads, and of the more massive *Pectinatella magnifica*, which form brown rosettes embedded shallowly in a mass of gelatinous secretion that may be bigger than a man's head.

The Lamp Shells *(Phylum Brachiopoda)*

The conspicuous parts of a lamp shell are its two shell valves, which fit tightly together like saucers facing one another. But unlike a bivalve mollusk, which has a right and a left valve, the valves of a lamp shell are dorsal and ventral.

In most of the 230 existing species of lamp shells, the lower valve extends beyond the region of the hinge and is perforated. Through the hole comes a short flexible stalk, which supports the animal on a rock or other firm object in the sea. The hole in an empty shell suggests that through which the wick of an oil lamp extended in Greek and Roman times; hence the name lamp shell.

The lamp shells of today are the dwindling remains of a phylum that is well represented in the fossil record ever since the early Cambrian period about 600 million years ago. Both the hingeless lamp shells (class Inarticulata) and those with hinge teeth that keep the shell valves aligned (class Articulata) have ancestries of equal length. Among the survivors of the Inarticulata are members of two genera that date from Ordovician times—many millions of years longer than any other genus of known animals. The older of the two, *Lingula*, is now limited to Indo-Pacific waters. Members of the other genus *(Crania)* are found cemented to rocks (by the ventral valve of the almost circular shell) along Atlantic coasts from the West Indies to Greenland and the English Channel. At higher latitudes, *Crania* lives in shallow water; near the Tropic of Cancer it finds conditions more suitable 600 feet below the surface. Another hingeless lamp shell, *Glottidia*, inhabits the intertidal sandy bottoms along American coasts from California to Peru and from the Carolinas around the Gulf of Mexico. Its shell valves may be 1 inch along, 2/5 inch wide, and its stalk may extend about 3/4 inch within the vertical burrow that the animal maintains in the sand.

The name of this phylum, brachiopod ("arm bearer"), refers to the two curled arms that support ciliated tentacles on each side of the mouth. These structures, and some similarities in embryonic development, lead zoologists to regard brachiopods as allied to the phyla Phoronida and Bryozoa. When a brachiopod holds its shell valves so that they gape a little, the cilia on the tentacles create two inbound currents of water, which later emerge as a central jet. Bacteria and other microscopic organic particles carried by the water are captured by a film of mucus on the tentacles. The loaded mucus is swallowed into a gut. In hingeless lamp shells this gut is U-shaped and ends in an anus but in members of the hinged group it ends blindly, requiring them to spit out pellets of undigested wastes.

The members of the hinged class of brachiopods are identified according to the shape of the shell valves and the degree of development of a symmetrical pair of limy loops that are located inside the dorsal valve and serve to support the tentacle-bearing arms. In *Terebratulina septentrionalis*, which is fairly

common along Atlantic coasts from Cape Cod northward and in waters of northern Europe, the limy loops resemble small stirrups in a pear-shaped shell about 1/2 inch long and 1/3 inch wide. *Terebratulina* can be discovered in Maine and Newfoundland by wading out during a minus tide. Along the Pacific coast at low-water mark, the reddish shells of *Terebratalia transversa* attain a width of 1-1/2 inches and enclose a much longer support loop. Additional crossbars bolster the limy loops of *Laqueus californianus*, which grows to a shell width of 2 inches on animals affixed to rocks in deep Pacific waters along coasts from southern California to Alaska and northern Japan.

The Mollusks *(Phylum Mollusca)*

The word mollusk (from the Latin *mollis*, meaning soft) refers to the living animal that secretes its shell, and to kindred kinds that are shell-less, such as slugs and octopuses. Of all the known kinds of animal life, almost a tenth are mollusks. Nearly as great a variety as are alive today is known from the fossil record, which extends back to the seas of early Cambrian times some 600 million years ago. Bivalves appear early among the fossils, along with uncoiled snail shells and the ancestors of today's chambered nautiluses.

Possibly more of the ancient kinds of mollusks will be discovered in the dark oceanic abysses. In 1957 the scientific world was startled to learn that bottom animals dredged from nearly 12,000 feet below the surface of the Pacific Ocean off the Nicaraguan coast included living representatives of mollusks known previously only from fossils of Cambrian to Devonian age. Named *Neopilina galatheae*, they were assigned to a new class (the Monoplacophora) because their bodies showed a series of paired muscles attached to the shell, paired gills and paired excretory tubules all suggesting a relationship to annelid worms without indicating actual segmentation. The collection in 1958 of a second species *(N. ewingi)* from more than 19,000 feet deep in the Peru-Chile Trench off northern Peru, reinforced a general belief that mollusks and annelids had a common ancestor during the Pre-Cambrian epoch. Similarities in embryonic development can be accounted for in the same way.

While evolving in directions that emphasized no segmental arrangements, the mollusks have developed many characteristic features. Dorsally and laterally these animals bear a fleshy tissue called the mantle, which secretes whatever

Hingless Lamp Shells (Glottidia pyrimidata)

limy shell they possess. Internally, the molluskan body includes a nervous system consisting commonly of three paired ganglia linked together. One lies above or beside the mouth, a second below the gullet, the center for nerves to the foot region, and a third, still more ventral, serves the mantle, gills, heart, and other visceral organs. Most mollusks possess a peculiar rasping organ called a radula, a ribbon-shaped tool that can be slid back and forth in the mouth, scraping free small particles of food. Differences in the development of the mantle, the foot, and the shell distinguish the six other classes of mollusks. All of them are represented in North America, along the coasts, in fresh waters, or on land.

The Sea Cradles (Class Amphineura)

Along the sea coast, members of this class of mollusks cling to rocks exposed at low tide, each animal with its oval, convex body protected by eight crosswise limy plates. Below is a firm body and a long flat foot that holds the rock tightly by suction. Its grip ends abruptly if a thin knife blade is slipped between the foot and the rock, breaking the seal and relieving the vacuum created by muscular contraction along the midline of the flat sole. Once freed, the sea cradle curls its body, and may roll over onto its back and rock gently like a cradle, just as its popular name suggests.

These animals are also known as chitons from a fancied resemblance to an ancient Greek garment that was held to the body by an encircling waist band. On the mollusk, the band or girdle is a portion of the mantle that is armored with small overlapping scales. Below it, along both sides of the foot, are 8 to 80 pairs of bushy gills. Yet this repetitive pattern, also found in the cross connections between the two separate but parallel nerve cords shows no correspondence that would indicate that a chiton is a segmented animal.

The largest of all sea cradles is *Cryptochiton stelleri*, which browses for algae on rocks along the Pacific coast from California to the Bering Straits and Japan. Its brick-red girdle completely hides its shell valves, and earns it the popular name of sea boot or gumboot. Average specimens extend for 10 inches, and giants are 13 inches long by 6 inches broad.

Much more common in the intertidal area along the Pacific shores is the black chiton *Katharina tunicata*, whose shiny black naked girdle covers most of its gray shell plates. Still more abundant and also 3 to 4 inches long is the sedentary

Nuttallina californica, which grows slowly and lives for perhaps 25 years in the same site. Gentle waves bring particles of organic matter, such as fragments of kelp, on which the mollusk feeds. Harsher waves pound the animal against the rock and slowly wear a depression in it. Apparently these are coveted sites, for if one *Nuttallina* is removed from a depression, another one or a mossy mopalia *(Mopalia muscosa)* of similar dimensions soon moves in and fills the vacancy. The girdle of the *Mopalia* bears stiff green hairs that give the appearance of a moss. Many algae and small animals of the fouling community take hold on a mopalia and grow there, increasing this illusion and camouflaging the mopalia from all but the most sharp-eyed beachcombers.

By comparison with more than 70 different kinds of sea cradles along the Pacific coast, including two dozen common ones, the number along the Atlantic shores and those of the Gulf of Mexico seems very small. *Acanthopleura granulata* of southern Florida, the Gulf coast, and the West Indies is almost alone in growing to a length of 3 inches. The more common ones are the northern red chiton *(Ischnochiton ruber),* found on Arctic coasts and as far south as Connecticut and central California, which rarely measures more than 1 inch even in the richest of tide pools, and the eastern chiton *(Chaetopleura apiculata),* found from New England to Florida, which has shell plates with rough, beadlike projections and a total length of seldom more than 3/4 inch. Skin divers find additional species in deeper water, both in northern regions where arctic kinds are numerous, and in southern Florida, where tropical species find suitable living conditions.

The Solenogasters (Class Aplacophora)

With 1-inch, wormlike bodies, these shell-less mollusks live at depths greater than 90 feet, either creeping over the hydroids and other marine cnidarians on which they feed, or burrowing shallowly in the muddy bottom. As these animals mature from the larval stage, they often lose their radula but develop a clothing of limy spicules that project through the enveloping mantle. *Chaetoderma nitidulum* lives along the New England coast.

The Snails and Slugs (Class Gastropoda)

Unlike an amphineuran or a *Neopilina,* in which the body shows bilateral symmetry, a snail or a slug develops a spiral form at an early age and retains

> *Overleaf: left, Lined Red Chiton (Tonicella lineata);*
> *right, Mossy Chiton (Mopalia muscosa)*

evidence of this twist for the rest of its life. Most of the spiral is seen in the body organs that are covered by the mantle, in the "visceral hump" on the back of the animal, usually under or within a one-piece shell. Seemingly this allows the creature to carry about a long, pointed mound of a body in a neatly portable form. The most astonishing feature of the gastropods is that so many members of this class of mollusks develop a spiral in the clockwise, or dextral, direction, as seen from the tip of the shell.

Snails and slugs appear to creep about on their belly surfaces; hence the class name (from the Greek *gaster* = belly, and *pes, podos* = foot). Their characteristic movement can be observed easily through a piece of transparent glass upon which a snail or slug is moving. The rim of the large flat foot skids along over a sheet of mucus secreted at the anterior end, while transverse bands of the sole alternately support the weight of the animal and move backward in a stretching action. Each band is then lifted clear of the mucus to shift forward again, ready to take part in the next downward cycle. Exceptional snails employ other methods of progression: the 1/3-inch chink shells *(Lacuna)* appear to waddle, advancing first one side of the narrow grooved foot and then the other; 3/4-inch salt marsh snails *(Melampus)* hitch themselves along, holding alternately with the forward and then the hinder portion of the foot; some of the 3-inch conchs *(Strombus)* almost leap along on a narrow foot armed with a sickle-like operculum.

Most gastropods are marine and possess the 180-degree twist in visceral parts that brings the gills, the excretory organs, the anus, and the mantle opening all into a forward-facing position. These characteristics are found in all members of the principal subclass (the Prosobranchiata—"the forward gilled" ones), in which the sexes are usually separate.

THE PROSOBRANCHS *(Subclass Prosobranchiata)*

The oldest and least specialized of the gastropods are the slit shells *(Pleurotomaria)* of a dozen kinds, of which two species live at depths of 700 feet or more in the Gulf of Mexico and around the southern tip of Florida. A beachcomber who finds one cast ashore after a violent storm has discovered a rarity. Far more common are the related top shells, turban shells, nerites (such as the "bleeding tooth," *Nerita peloronta*), the various types of limpets found in the intertidal zone on rocky coasts, and the ear shells (or abalones, *Haliotis*) found at slightly greater depths, particularly along the California shore.

The top shells (such as *Margarites*, *Calliostoma*, and *Tegula*), like the turban

Limpets (Acmaea digitalis)

shells *(Turbo)* and the nerites, gain some safety by producing thick, sturdy shells and being able to close the door after withdrawing inside with a horny operculum carried on the upper surface of the foot. Limpets *(Acmaea)* and keyhole limpets *(Fissurella)* dispense with an operculum as they grow and instead rely upon being able to cling to a rock more tightly than any other motile animal of comparable size. The suction grip of an alarmed limpet has been measured and found to be as great as 70 pounds per square inch.

Only the first tiny whorl or two of a limpet's shell shows its spiral nature. Thereafter, as the animal grows, its mantle spreads out tentlike and enlarges the shell all around at a fairly uniform rate, making it almost bilaterally symmetrical. A keyhole limpet (or "volcano shell") leaves an unfilled notch in the edge of its original small shell, and this gap becomes the hole at the peak as enlargement makes the shell symmetrical. The keyhole limpet continues to use the opening for discharge of digestive wastes and of water drawn under the rim of the shell at the anterior end by cilia that cover the surface of the mantle.

The dunce-cap limpet *(Acmaea mitra)* of the Pacific coast from Mexico to Alaska is the tallest of the true limpets. Large ones are close to 2 inches long and 1 inch high. The owl limpet *(Lottia gigantia)*, which is common on rocks at tide line from California to Mexico, is much larger, often reaching a length of 4 inches but only 1 inch in height. Along Atlantic coasts, the limpets are smaller. The Atlantic plate limpet *(A. testudinalis)* is common in the intertidal zone of New England waters; this one-inch mollusk ranges northward to the Arctic and down cold shores of Europe. It is obviously different from the spotted limpet *(A. pustulata)* of southeastern Florida, the Gulf of Mexico and the West Indies, which has radiating ridges.

Of the eight different kinds of abalones along the Pacific coast from British Columbia to Mexico, the black species *(Haliotis cracherodi)* is most conspicuously a denizen of the surf. It clings to rock ledges through which waves plunge, keeping its shell clean and shining, and its 5 to 9 perforations conspicuous while it grows to 7 inches in greatest diameter. Apparently it feeds on microscopic plants brought to it by the sea, whereas other abalones take larger fare. The green abalone *(H. fulgens)* seems particularly quick in reacting when a wave brings a piece of seaweed into momentary contact with the long tentacles

Kelp Limpets (Acmaea incessa) on Egregia

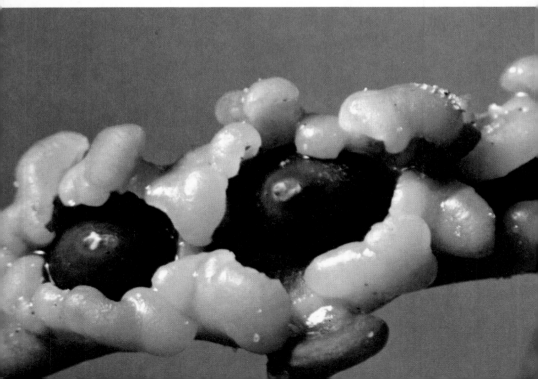

Pacific Top Shell (Calliostoma ligatum)

that project under its mantle edge; it whirls and uses the anterior edge of its foot to clamp the seaweed to the rock until its mouth can be brought to bear upon the nourishment and its radula rasp off pieces small enough to swallow. The slightly larger red abalone *(H. rufescens)*, which is reputed to have the best flavor of these edible animals, generally supports a heavy incrustation of algae, hydroids, and moss animals. So eagerly are the red abalones sought that a minimum size for legal possession has now been set at 7 inches, which may correspond to about 12 years of age. Apparently these animals begin to breed at 6 years and a length of about 4 inches, but their reproduction can scarcely keep up with the rate of commercial harvesting.

Evolution has produced an intermediate group of prosobranch gastropods that have lost one kidney and one gill but are so well adapted to living conditions in a host of different habitats that they include more than half of the known species of all mollusks. Some of them, such as the slipper shells *(Crepidula)* that are found along all American coasts and the strictly littoral periwinkles

(Littorina), are vegetarians. Slipper shells tend to take up permanent residence wherever the coastal sea water contains plenty of plankton. This may be in the doorway of a snail, on the shell of a horseshoe crab, or atop another slipper shell—until a mass of as many as 40 lies as a cluster on the sea floor. A particularly common species from the Atlantic coast of North America, *C. fornicata*, was introduced accidentally in Puget Sound, and also in northern Europe, where it has become a pest that smothers oysters. Each *Crepidula* holds to its oval, boat-shaped shell by a horizontal shelf across the posterior end inside, a feature that leads to the name of slipper or "quarter-deck shell." To feed, the animal spreads a thin film of mucus over the sides of its foot and waits for particles of nourishment to become embedded in it. At intervals of about four minutes, the mollusk twists its head to the side and sucks up the loaded mucus. It swallows small particles immediately but stores larger ones in a pouch at the front of the mouth, seemingly as emergency rations to be eaten when it must clamp its shell down tight.

Periwinkles wander about, using a long coiled radula to get particles of food. Some of them are the most common snails on and under rockweeds at low tide. In addition to about 20 different species native to American coasts, the "winkle" *(L. littorea)* that Europeans regard as eminently edible is now abundant from Labrador to Maryland. Apparently it came with the Norsemen to Newfoundland but did not cross the Gulf of St. Lawrence until 1840, when it was discovered at Pictou, Nova Scotia. It reached Halifax (1857), St. John, New Brunswick (1861), Portland, Maine (1870), New Haven, Connecticut (1879), Atlantic City, New Jersey (1892), and Cape May (1928), and now is found south of the open end of Chesapeake Bay. It clings to seaweeds in the intertidal zone, or spends the hours of ebb tide on rocks and in tide pools. At high tide, it scrapes diatoms and other microscopic algae from rocks, pilings, underwater vegetation, and mud flats. So far, it has not reached Californian coasts, where the 1/2-inch checkered periwinkle *(L. scutulata)* is often alone but sometimes accompanied by the eroded periwinkle *(L. planaxis)*. Both species range to Alaska and are joined by others from the cold waters of Puget Sound northward. Among them is one of the smallest (1/4 to 1/2 inch), known as the rough periwinkle *(L. saxatilis)*, which lives also around the Arctic Ocean and down the North Atlantic seaboard to New Jersey and is almost terrestrial. Often it clings to rocks above high tide mark, or feeds on seashore lichens during wet weather.

Snails of related families live in fresh water, but not on land. *Amnicola* and

Moon Snail (Polinices sp.)
"Sea Collar" egg mass of Atlantic Moon Snail (Polinices duplicata)

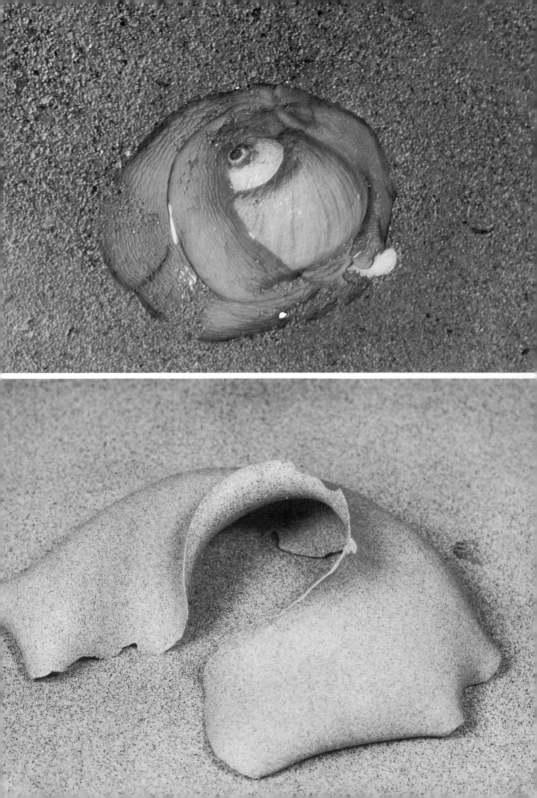

Bulimus (family Amnicolidae) creep about on very short feet, bearing broad shells, among pondweeds or on sandy bottoms. *Vivipara* (Viviparidae), with a larger, globose shell and longer foot, is found on muddy bottoms of both lakes and slow rivers. *Valvata* (Valvatidae), with prominent keels or ridges on 1/4-inch shells, extend an extraordinarily large feathery gill while moving about in lakes, both in shallow and fairly deep water. *Goniobasis* (Pleuroceridae) feeds on aquatic plants near lake shores and in rapid rivers, producing a long, conical shell with seven or more whorls.

In the sea, carnivorous snails of many types have arisen in this intermediate group of prosobranchs. Among the strangest are the pelagic violet snails *(Janthina)* that are frequently cast ashore along Pacific shores and Florida's eastern coast, each snail still clinging to a tough, transparent float composed of gas bubbles with gelatinous walls. This particular species *(J. janthina)* is ovoviparous, but others in tropical waters use the float to support their fertilized eggs. The shells of these snails are extremely thin and delicate, and of a pale pastel hue that probably makes them inconspicuous while close to the surface of the open ocean. It is there that the snail uses its long, prehensile proboscis to spear small medusae or to feed on the by-the-wind sailor *(Velella)* and Portuguese man-of-war *(Physalia)* colonies.

Another prize for the beachcomber is a "sea collar," composed of sand grains, mucus and tiny eggs of a moon snail *(Lunatia,* or *Polinices)*. This active, predatory snail spreads mucus and eggs together over its greatly expanded foot, and waits until the mucus, mixed with sand from the sea floor, hardens somewhat before it glides out through a gap at the anterior end. Otherwise, moon snails plow through the sand in search of bivalve mollusks around which they can wrap their foot and hold firmly. Using the radula as a file, they cut an opening through the bivalve's shell and reach in to cut up their prey into particles that can be sucked out and swallowed.

The giant helmet shells *(Cassis)*, found from North Carolina to the Gulf of Mexico, the West Indies and Brazilian waters, feed on bivalves and sea urchins. Largest is the emperor, or queen, helmet *(C. madagascariensis)*, which attains a length of 14 inches and a weight of more than 5 pounds. This, and the smaller king helmet *(C. tuberosa)*, are commonly collected for shipment to Europe as the raw material from which engravers can make cameo jewelry.

Fig shells, such as the common *Ficus communis* from North Carolina to Mexico, specialize in eating sea urchins and other echinoderms which they search out in sand bars and beaches under shallow seas. Tritons of various

Intertidal Rock Shells (Thais) with egg cases
Preceding page: top left, Chestnut Cowries (Cypraea spadicea); bottom, Hawk-wing Conch (Strombus raninus); right, Flamingo Tongue (Cyphoma gibbosum)

genera feed on sea stars, or starfishes. A 4-inch triton, *Fusitriton oregonensis*, is common on rocky and sandy bottoms at depths from 20 to 200 feet along the Pacific coast from southern California to Alaska. Both smaller and larger kinds are numerous in intertidal waters and to greater depths along shores of the southeastern United States, through the West Indies, to South America. The giant is triton's trumpet *(Charonia variegata)*, which lives in crevices of coral reefs and attains a length of 10 inches or more. Like similar shells from waters around other continents, it is a favorite of fishermen, who drill a small hole in the side of the spire and then blow through it to produce a sound like a bugle. Shinto priests in Japan use it as a call to worship.

Cowries *(Cypraea)* may be more versatile. The chestnut cowrie *(C. spadicea)*, which ranges along the Pacific coast from Monterey to Baja, California, has been observed in the low-tide zone feeding on small anemones, sponges, certain colonial tunicates, the egg masses of other snails, a dead abalone, and perhaps the algal film on rocks. The thin mantle of a cowrie is generally raised so high along both sides of the smooth shell that the handsome pattern is hidden; instead, the mantle exhibits fleshy tubercles and warts that help the snail blend with its surroundings. At a touch, however, the mantle shrinks away, exposing the shiny shell and preparing to withdraw completely through the narrow aperture along the underside. In Atlantic and Gulf waters, tropical cowries of several kinds are fairly common among corals on shallow reefs and near protective rocks in shallow water.

Herbivorous habits and scavenging for meat are both shown by conchs *(Strombus)*, of which nearly a dozen different kinds range from southeastern Florida through the West Indies and around the Gulf of Mexico to South America. The pink, or queen, conch *(S. gigas)* creeps about among the turtle-grass and over sandy bottoms. Its shell, 10 inches long when fully grown, has a broad wing that hides the narrow foot from above. Smaller "fighting" conchs, such as *S. alatus*, 3 inches long, have become famous for their pugnacity when placed together in an aquarium. All of these carnivores have especially well-developed eyes on movable stalks, each stalk ending in a short sensitive tentacle. Fishermen in tropical waters often use the tough flesh of conchs as bait because it cannot easily be torn from a hook, or to flavor chowders when fishing is poor.

The most advanced of the prosobranch snails are all marine. They include the rock shells, oyster drills, whelks, mud snails, the 18-inch Florida horse conch *(Pleuroploca gigantea)*, which is among the largest of all snails, and the cone shells, some species of which can be deadly to those who handle them. All of

Channeled Whelk (Busycon canaliculata) with its string of eggs

115

Garden Snail (Helix aspersa)
116

them have a special notch or canal through which the slender siphon is extended to get water and sample it for possible food.

American species of *Murex* and other genera in the rock-shell family (Muricidae) almost all produce from a gland in the mantle a yellowish, ill-smelling fluid that can in sunlight become the deep lavender dye called Tyrian purple. This dye is virtually identical with the substance obtained from *Murex* snails in Mediterranean waters and known as "royal purple" because of its use by kings in ancient times. Probably the secretion is used by the snail to anesthetize the bivalves and chitons upon which it normally preys. Surprisingly, the snail itself can swim as well as creep rapidly, despite a medium-weight shell; the shell has ornamental ribs and spines and an elongated siphon canal.

Oyster drills *(Urosalpinx)* are among the most common of small (3/4-inch) snails along the Atlantic coast from the Gulf of St. Lawrence to Florida and rank along with sea stars (starfish) as the most devastating predators on oysters, mussels, and other bivalves. The Atlantic species *U. cinerea* has, unfortunately, been introduced in northern Europe and along the Pacific coast from Washington to California, where related species were not quite so serious a pest to shell-fishermen. The larger whelks, *Busycon*, attack large bivalves, force open the shell of each victim and wedge it agape by inserting the edge of its own shell into it. The whelk then reaches with its long proboscis deep into the bivalve and eats out the soft parts. *Busycon* egg strings, known as sea necklaces, consist of many flat packets each containing from 20 to 100 developing embryos, along one side of a tough connecting strand one end of which is anchored deeply in the sea floor. The smaller whelks, *Buccinum*, and the mud snails, *Nassa and Nassarius*, by contrast, are scavengers that consume dead fishes or other carrion, thus converting it into fresh snail meat that is eaten, shell and all, by cod and haddock.

Cone shells *(Conus)* do not wait for fishes to die. They watch alertly until a fish comes close and then shoot it with a special radular dart connected to a poison gland. Another snail or a marine worm is equally suitable as a target and a meal. So far, no human deaths from "bites" of American cone shells have been confirmed, but fatalities are well known in the Indo-Pacific region. California has one species, *C. californicus*, with a smooth, brown shell about 1 inch long. The Atlantic and Gulf coasts have two species, *C. floridanus*, 1 inch, and *C. jaspideus stearnsi*, 1/2 inch, that range from North Carolina southward, and about 10 others of the Caribbean region that appear in warm shallows of the Florida Keys.

THE PULMONATES *(Subclass Pulmonata)*

Possession of a special pocket—a "lung"—in the mantle tissue, opening to the outside world by a pore that can be dilated or constricted, is the most distinctive feature by which about 8,000 different snails and slugs are grouped together in the subclass Pulmonata. Only a few, such as the saltmarsh snail *(Melampus)*, which attains 1/2 inch in length, found from the Gulf of St. Lawrence to the Gulf of Mexico, are associated with the sea—and *Melampus* generally climbs a salt grass stem to stay just beyond the reach of high tide. The other members of the subclass are denizens of fresh water or are terrestrial and surprisingly intolerant of salt for animals whose ancestors must have come from the marine world.

The freshwater snails climb or float upward to the water surface to open their lung for a breath of air and then descend to browse on aquatic vegetation. The most common types are widespread and easy to identify by shape. The bulkiest is the apple snail *(Pomacea paludas)*, 2 inches in each dimension, found in ponds and ditches of the southeastern United States. Those in the Florida Everglades are the favorite food of the limpkin and virtually the only item of diet of the rare Everglades kite. Pond snails with a pointed spire and a shell 2-1/2 inches long are *Lymnaea stagnalis*, a species found in quiet waters also in Eurasia. An introduced European species, *L. auricularis*, with a huge body whorl is now spreading in the eastern United States. Small, generally dark brown snails, with a left-handed spiral instead of a right, are tadpole snails *(Physa)*. Wheel snails *(Helisoma)* have the spiral almost all in the same plane and carry the shell vertically above the back. The freshwater limpet *(Ferrissia)* is unusual in having a conical gill as well as a lung, and it is easy to overlook because it is less than 1/3 inch long. All of these snails possess a single pair of sensitive tentacles, which are solid and cannot be withdrawn; at the base of each is an eye, flush with the surface of the head.

Land snails and slugs, by contrast, bear their eyes at the tip of a second, longer, upper pair of tentacles. These can be retracted, turning outside-in like a glove finger and thus pulling the eye to safety in the head. If, however, some animal nips off an eye-bearing tentacle, the mollusk can regenerate a new one.

Except in the southernmost part of Florida, no native land snails in the United States or Canada attain the size of the Roman or edible snail *(Helix pomatia)* that has long been a favored delicacy in Europe. Live snails of this species have been imported for sale, but have formed wild colonies so far only in Ohio.

118   *Pond Snails (Limnaea)*

Black Slugs (Limax) mating and eggs hatching

*Overleaf: left, Purple Nudibranch (Flabellinopsis iodinea); top right,
White Nudibranch (Diaulula sandiegensis); center right, White Nudibranch
(Dirona albolineata); bottom right, Translucent Nudibranch (Melibe leonina)*

Two European relatives that have settled on both coasts, often to the dismay of market gardeners upon whose crops they feed, are the garden snail *(Cepaea hortensis)* and the grove snail *(C. nemoralis)*, which are almost an inch in diameter and have a yellow to brown or reddish shell, often with encircling bands of brownish black.

In southern Florida, both on the Keys and isolated higher areas with tropical and subtropical trees in the Everglades, tree snails *(Liguus)* appear to be native. Each colony tends to have its own color pattern, although all eat approximately the same foods—chiefly fungi and lichens that coat tree bark. It seems likely that *Liguus* was blown to these sites and to the island of Cozumel from Cuba during hurricanes, since this is the total range of the species. The chance that a violent wind could whirl them unharmed through the sky for a distance of 150 miles on rare occasions is increased by the habit shown by *Liguus* during extended periods of dry or cold weather. The snail cements itself firmly by the rim of its shell to tree branches and is not easily dislodged.

Slugs differ from land snails chiefly in having a smaller visceral hump and in protecting themselves with more copious quantities of mucus. In *Limax*, and some related genera, a small shell is concealed in the mantle tissue. In *Arion* the shell is dispensed with entirely at an early stage of development. Both native species and several from nothern Europe have been introduced widely in North America. Generally they are active at night, leaving trails of mucus that glisten until dried by the sun or coated with dust. A slug that is pecked by a bird may eject multiple jets of milky slime for a distance equal to its own length; for *Limax maximus*, this distance may be as great as 8 inches.

THE OPISTHOBRANCHS (Subclass Opisthobranchiata)

These are the least well known scientifically of the gastropods, and are grouped together because all of them start out producing a shell with a left-hand spiral and then usually stop, or even obliterate the shell entirely. Many dispense with a radula, or lack gills or a mantle cavity. Those that have the ordinary type of breathing organs for marine mollusks usually have only one gill and, like the mantle cavity, it extends to one side of the rear (hence "opistho") because the body organs have undergone a "detorsion" after developing a spiral twist like that of a prosobranch.

The most bizarre of opisthobranchs that beachcombers and skin divers encounter are surely the nudibranchs—sometimes called sea slugs. Lacking a mantle cavity, shell, and true gills as adults, they make use of the body surface and special projections, called cerata, from the mantle as respiratory organs. Creeping over seaweeds and coralline growths, or swimming by vigorous and graceful undulations of the long foot, they can reach hydroids, bryozoans, and snail eggs which they use as food. Most nudibranchs have fanciful colors, with decorative tufts of cerata, or, if they bear the anus on the dorsal surface toward the rear, have a whorl of plumelike secondary gills there. Members of genera referred to as eolids possess the strange ability to digest all of a coelenterate except its stinging cells (nematocysts) and to transfer these cells intact and undischarged into the surface tissues of the mollusk's body. An eolid, such as a Coryphella, can then use the hydroid's weapons long after the coelenterate itself has been absorbed as food. Other nudibranchs probably rely upon their extremely disagreeable flavor for protection; almost no animal will eat them.

The red-fingered eolis *(Coryphella rufibranchialis)*, an inch long and fringed above with slender cerata, is common in the intertidal zone from the Arctic to Long Island Sound. The frond eolis *(Dendronotus frondosus)*, which is twice as long and decked with branching cerata, has a similar range and also occurs down the Pacific coast to Puget Sound. Humm's polycera *(Polycera hummi)*, 1/3 inch long, glides among the eelgrass meadows between North Carolina and Florida. It has four tentacles on its head and four cerata behind the dorsal branchial plume marked in consecutive rings of bright blue and orange. On wharf pilings along the West Coast, an orange-yellow dorid *(Anisodoris nobilis)* with a frilly white branchial plume attains a length of 4 inches. A still more fanciful nudibranch, *Glaucus marina*, in various shades of blue and with clumps of dark blue cerata outstretched along each side, is often washed ashore from warm waters of the Gulf of Mexico; it is a pelagic species that creeps about below the surface film of the open ocean.

Pelagic opisthobranchs include a whole order of pteropods (Pteropoda), or sea butterflies, mostly less than 1/2 inch in length, in which the anterior portion of the foot is expanded into a pair of winglike swimming organs. Members of species that lack a shell of any kind seem to be predators, actively hunting out minute animals among the plankton. *Clione limacina* attains a length of 1-1/2 inches on this diet in North Atlantic waters and, in turn, becomes food for the Greenland whale and other baleen whales. Pteropods with shells appear to gather diatoms and similarly microscopic organisms into a film of mucus secreted by the swimming lobes and conveyed to the mouth by cilia; gizzard teeth crush the skeletal material. Although members of *Limacina* and *Clavolina* can often be collected close to American shores in a fine net towed behind a

Overleaf: top left, Belligerent Dorid (Phidiana pugnax); bottom left, Carpenter's Dorid (Triopha carpenteri); right, Nudibranch eggs (Anisodoris sp.)

small boat, these and other related pteropods are common in cold waters from the Arctic to the Antarctic, but at greater depths close to the Equator. Shells of dead pteropods give character to "pteropod ooze" upon the sea floor near the mid-Atlantic ridge, particularly in low latitudes.

Largest of the opisthobranchs are the sea hares, such as the common yellow to olive-green *Aplysia californica*, 5 to 15 inches long, which feeds on seaweeds along the Pacific coast. These animals have an internal vestige of a shell, which is completely hidden by the large fleshy folds of the mantle. If disturbed, a sea hare gives off a great flood of purple fluid which seems harmless, although it may repel predators that hunt by olfactory sense in the marine world.

Spiral limy shells are formed by opisthobranchs in several families known as bubble shells and as pyrams. But most of these mollusks lack a radula and feed instead either as predators—sucking in small victims and crushing them with gizzard teeth—or as parasites, inserting a slender proboscis and sucking out

Sea Hare (Elysia bedeckta) with spiral of eggs

the juices from sedentary animals. One group known as sacoglossids, has become worldwide (with about 50 species) as a saltwater counterpart to aphids. They cling to seaweeds and suck nourishment from one plant cell after another.

Perhaps the strangest of all gastropods are the members of the genus *Berthelinea* that have been found browsing on the common tropical green alga *Caulerpa*. The Caribbean species, *B. caribbea*, is about 1/5 inch long, green with yellow streaks; the southern California kind, *B. chloris*, is slightly larger and bright green. Upon their backs, concealing the posterior end of the foot, these peculiar animals wear a bivalved shell, hinge uppermost. The left valve has a coiled apex.

The Bivalves (Class Pelecypoda)

In North America, the most popular mollusks for human food are clams, scallops, and oysters, in all of which the outer surface of the mantle secretes

Atlantic Jacknife Clam (Ensis directus)

a two-part shell—a left valve and a right. The hinge ligament may be assisted by limy teeth that resist any force tending to get the two valves out of perfect alignment. This region of the shell grows most slowly, while concentric enlargements are made around the rim elsewhere. Generally, the shell has three layers: an outer horny covering that protects the structure from erosion; an intermediate region composed of calcium carbonate crystals in tightly packed prisms; and an inner layer known as "mother-of-pearl" in which extremely thin films of lime crystals alternate with equally thin films of horny material, providing a diffraction of reflected light that confers an intriguing iridescence. The mantle tissue generally reacts to any grain of sand or small animal that gets between it and the shell by coating the foreign object with mother-of-pearl. Progressively this process enlarges the irritating object as a pearl, which may be spherical but more often is irregular.

The rate at which a bivalve enlarges its shell varies considerably, being fastest when food is plentiful and slowest when the surrounding water is depleted, cold, or made turbid by a storm. Changes in rate tend to be recorded in the concentric grooves and ridges that mark the external surface of the shell. In areas where growth is slow at only one season of each year and no storms have muddied the water all through the period of active feeding, the shell may show annual markings by which an expert can determine the age of the animal.

In all pelecypods, the body structure seems simplified toward an emphasis on drawing water with oxygen and food particles into the mantle cavity, capturing the particles in a film of mucus that cilia can move to the mouth, and expelling the water again with wastes and perhaps the products of the reproductive organs. No pelecypod has a head or a radula, but its foot may be bladelike and extensile as an organ of locomotion. Pelecypoda is derived from the Greek words *pelekys*, a hatchet, and *pes* (genitive *podos*) a foot. This way of life is unsuited to terrestrial existence or aerial activity. In the aquatic world, however, it has been developed by about 7,000 different kinds of animals for plowing along in a muddy bottom without getting stuck, excavating a secluded chamber in firmer sediments or timber or rock, tethering the body temporarily to a solid substratum, leaping over the sandy floor of the sea, creeping up a plant stem, swimming to escape a predatory sea star, cementing one valve permanently to the bottom and living indolently ever after, or lying quietly embedded in a coral reef under a tropical sun while raising microscopic plants as food.

Along the margins of small lakes and slow streams, fishermen often notice the discarded shell valves of the papershell clam *(Anodonta gracilis)*, as much

Atlantic Bay Scallop (Aequipecten irradians)

131

as 6 inches long, that have been dropped by raccoons, muskrats, or mink. Bathers wading barefoot where the water is 2 to 4 feet deep are more likely to see the furrow left in the bottom or to step on the live bivalve. Even in the tributaries of the Mississippi River and lesser drainage systems in the eastern half of North America, the larger freshwater clams rarely live at depths greater than 6 feet. One called the freshwater mussel *(Elliptio crassidens)*, with a heavy shell as much as 6 inches long, was exploited for many years as a major source of raw material from which to cut "pearl" buttons. The tiny fingernail clams, such as *Sphaerium*, rarely as much as 1/2 inch across, glide up and down plant stems as smoothly as though they were snails instead of pelecypods with a slender, adhesive foot. All of these denizens of fresh waters either retain their fertilized eggs in an ovoviviparous habit or release specialized larvae called glochidia. Each glochidium has a pair of small shell valves, held widely spread, ending in tonglike hooks. The larval bivalve uses them to pinch into the skin of a passing fish or to hold to the gills when it is taken into the mouth. The glochidium thereupon becomes a temporary parasite, absorbing nourishment while growing; eventually it drops to the bottom, wherever the fish chances to be, and transforms into the adult body style of its species. In this way the freshwater bivalves make use of the ability of fishes to stay in fresh water without being carried by the current to the sea.

Most marine bivalves, by contrast, go through larval stages as minute drifting members of the plankton. This habit attends to the dispersal of the economically important oysters (*Crassostrea virginica* along the Atlantic coast, *C. gigas* on Pacific shorelines and in Japan, intertidally and at greater depths), which settle as "spat" and cement their left valves to a support. Swimming larvae serve in the same way the soft-shell clams *(Mya)* of Atlantic and Arctic shallows, which is a favorite for New England chowders and clambakes, a principal item of diet for the walrus in the Far North, and a shellfish that was introduced accidentally along Pacific shores in attempts to transplant Atlantic oysters to the West Coast. The soft-shell and the popular quahog (hard-shell, little-neck, or cherrystone clam, *Mercenaria mercenaria*) live subtidally in beaches where the sand is mixed with mud and provides a firm medium in which to maintain a short vertical burrow. The posterior end of the mantle in these pelecypods extends as a siphon or "neck" that can be protruded slightly to take in and discharge water or be quickly jerked down to safety at the slightest disturbance or when exposed by a low tide. The burrowing habit attains its greatest development in the edible geoduck [pronounced goo'ee-duck] of Puget Sound and adjacent coasts from

British Columbia to northern California. The 8-inch shell of a geoduck *(Panope generosa)* accounts for only a small part of the weight of this mollusk, which may reach 12 pounds, for the siphons are almost as large as the body proper and enable the bivalve to live 3 or 4 feet below the surface of the muddy bottom. The body itself grows too large for the shells to cover, and they suggest the wings of a bird whose breast is the thick, fleshy (and delectable) mantle of the geoduck.

With a slight change in habit, certain bivalves have become borers in sandstone, cement breakwaters, and timbers of many kinds from ship bottoms to wharf pilings. The Arctic rock borer *(Hiatella arctica,* formerly *Saxicava)* excavates a hole for itself about three times as long as its 2-inch shell valves, from low-water line to 600 feet below the surface, and along both coasts from the tropics to the Arctic but more shallowly in colder water. Boring bivalves of the family Pholadidae, known as angel wings *(Pholas)*, piddocks *(Zirphaea)* and martesias *(Martesia)* include nearly 40 different kinds along American coasts, particularly the Pacific and Gulf of Mexico shorelines. Because martesias make homes for themselves in floating timbers and wooden ships, in much the same way as the shipworms *(Teredo)* of family Teredinidae, they have become almost cosmopolitan in warm waters. Often they become captives in their own burrows, able to enlarge only the cavity around their bodies and not the slender entrance passage through which they continue to extend their siphons for intake of water and discharge of wastes and reproductive products. Usually a shipworm's burrow follows the grain of the wood, turning aside only to avoid a knot or a neighboring shipworm. Eventually the timber breaks apart, causing a dock to collapse or a ship to founder.

AGILE COCKLES AND SWIMMING BIVALVES
(Families Cardiidae, Pectinidae, and Limidae)

The heart-shaped cockles (family Cardiidae) have such short siphons that a half-buried position in a sandy bottom is about as deep as the mollusk can go. It is easily washed from its position by a strong current or a wave. It is then likely to kick itself along for a few yards before using its narrow, pointed foot to find a new place to stay. Often a fish swallows a cockle whole, or a storm tosses it high on shore to die. Beachcombers who step on cockleshells note their brittleness. Some, such as the Atlantic cockle *(Dinocardium robustum)* of southeastern coasts and the Gulf of Mexico, are stronger and 4 inches in each direction. Some of the Pacific species, such as *Clinocardium nuttalli*, found from

133

California to Alaska, are equally large and durable. The Iceland cockle *(C. ciliatum)*, only 2 inches long, is often very common from Cape Cod to the Arctic Ocean and down the West Coast to Puget Sound.

Scallops (family Pectinidae) are even more active, but have a foot too short to be used in locomotion. Instead, they gobble their way through the water, taking it in around the scalloped margin of the shell and expelling it in little jets through the "ears" at the hinge line. The edges of the mantle serve as valves in controlling this flow and also bear many bright little eyes with which a scallop can keep informed of objects moving near by. If a scallop chances to settle on its left valve, it generally rights itself at once. All of these movements are controlled by a single large muscle, which is the short, cylindrical morsel that gourments enjoy when it has been prepared for the table.

New Englanders have a strong preference for the Atlantic bay scallop *(Aequipecten irradians)*, which grows to be 3 inches across and is found in eelgrass shallows between Nova Scotia and Long Island Sound; their muscle tissue is particularly delicate in texture and flavor. From New Jersey to Colombia, the same species lives in deeper water, with smaller and more convex shells to which subspecific names have been given. The commercial scallops, *Placopecten magellanicus* between North Carolina and Labrador, and *Pecten caurinus* from California to Alaska, are more usually the deep-sea species, harvested between 200 and 300 feet below the surface, with 8-inch shells and heavier, coarser muscles.

Among rocks and corals in warm waters around southeastern Florida, two different kinds of file shells *(Lima)* swim in and out of favored "nest" sites, each mollusk growing to be 2 inches long with slender tactile tentacles extending all around the gaping margin. File shells use a gland on a short foot to secrete special threads with which to line their nest cavities, which usually are open at both ends. While in residence, these little bivalves create a feeding current that enters at one doorway and leaves at the other.

THE TETHERED MUSSELS AND PEN SHELLS
(Families Mytilidae and Pinnidae)

Threadlike or bristly strands of horny material that are secreted by a gland on the foot constitute the byssus with which a mussel, a pen shell and some other pelecypods anchor themselves firmly in place. Since marine mussels *(Mytilus* and *Modiolus)* are generally the most common bivalves along temperate and Arctic coastlines between mid tide and somewhat below low tide, the advantages

Arrow Squids mating (Loligo opalescens)

of a byssus seem evident. It enables each of these elongate, narrow-ended mollusks to retain its place in a dense cluster on a rock, on a wharf piling, or in a continuous carpet over sand bars and mud flats. Yet if the supply of food particles brought by the tidal waters diminishes seriously, any young or middle-aged mussel can move off to a new location. Carefully it stretches out its foot, attaches a fresh byssal strand as far as it can reach, lets go of its old byssus, and repeats the process. In a day or two it can progress several feet in a moderately straight line, leaving a trail of abandoned byssal strands.

Pen shells *(Pinna and Atrina)* anchor themselves with the pointed end deep in muddy sand. Although the small foot attaches its secreted strands to whatever buried stones and broken shells are within reach, the force of a storm on the exposed portion of the thin, fan-shaped shell valves may be too great. Churning waves can free thousands of 6- to 8-inch pen shells from their moorings and cast them among the beach drift to die. The small crabs *(Pinnotheres)* and some segmented worms that hide and feed in the mantle cavity of these shells must

135

then find new homes or perish too. Often the beachcomber finds them still in place. With luck, a person can discover in a dying pen shell one of the fine black pearls that they produce. These opportunities come unexpectedly, but can be watched for along sandy coasts from North Carolina to the Caribbean and around the Gulf of Mexico.

The Tusk Shells (Class Scaphopoda)

Among the treasures cast upon the shore from intertidal waters or depths of 600 feet or more are occasional tusk shells, each a limy tapering tube with a slight curvature, open at both ends. While occupied by the mollusk that secretes it, the shell is half or almost entirely buried in a sandy bottom, and is slanted to keep the smaller end exposed. There water enters and leaves the shell, attending to the respiratory needs of the animal while from the larger,

Common Atlantic Octopus (Octopus vulgaris)

lower opening it extends a foot resembling a horse's hoof, used as a digging organ, and a number of slender ciliated tentacles that probe the sand for small animals as food to be brought to the mouth.

Most of the 200 different American species of tusk shells live at depths of 500 feet or more and are rarely seen. Distinctive features in the shells at the small end help to identity them. One 2-inch species, *Dentalium eboreum*, lives in the intertidal zone between North Carolina and the Caribbean. A larger kind, *D. pretiosum*, along Pacific coasts north from Mexico was once used by western Indians as a medium for barter. A 2-inch shell had a purchasing power somewhat greater than a modern dollar. Rare 3-inch shells were owned only by the wealthy chiefs, who wore them around the neck on a cord.

The Cephalopods (Class Cephalopoda)

All of these mollusks are marine predators. Apparently their ancestors have always followed this way of life, at least since early Cambrian times. During the intervening 600 million years, the number of kinds that produce an external shell has dwindled to just three species in the genus *Nautilus*, now found exclusively in the tropical Indo-Pacific region. Yet the cup-shaped or conical mantle of the octopuses and squids has changed little to match the loss or reduction and enclosure of the shell. The mouth of these animals is always surrounded by a mass that represents the molluskan foot, although it is extended into a cluster of 8 or more flexible, muscular tentacles. The prey, such as a crab or fish, is seized with these and thrust into the mouth. There a pair of horny jaws, somewhat resembling the beak of a parrot, cut up the victim into fragments that the radula can readily shred. Digestion continues in a U-shaped gut. All of this structure emphasizes the head of the animal, making the cephalopod "head footed."

Few of the surviving 400 species of cephalopods live where they can be encountered readily by land-based men. The squids tend to move into deeper waters by day, and the octopuses to hide in favorite lairs. Both types of animals watch their world with camera-style eyes that are amazingly similar anatomically to those of vertebrates, although quite different in embryonic origin.

The long-finned squids (*Loligo pealei* from the Gulf of St. Lawrence to the West Indies, and *L. opalescens* from Puget Sound to southern California) attain a length of 2 feet and have large eyes, whereas the short-finned squid (*Illex illecebrosus*) of the same Atlantic waters is slightly smaller, with small eyes. All of these animals are caught commercially for fish bait and some are used as human food under the table name of calamary. At night, as schools of squids are pursuing small fishes, they sometimes dart tailfirst into air and drop onto rafts or into dories at their moorings.

The octopuses, with 8 sucker-studded arms instead of 10, swim less often and less vigorously, but equally well by jet propulsion by means of water ejected through a nozzle-like structure from the mantle cavity. From Connecticut southward, the Atlantic octopus *(Octopus vulgaris)* grows to a length of about 24 inches. On the Pacific coast, the common octopus is *O. hongkongensis*, which is rarely larger than 36 inches long in Californian waters but attains a length of as much as 14 feet along Alaskan shores and then is smaller in size again at lower latitudes near coasts of temperate Asia.

At greater depths or distances from land, other cephalopods lead active lives without being noticed. Occasionally, the deep purple, 3-foot umbrella octopus *(Tremoctopus violaceus)*, whose distribution is as worldwide as the warm-water Portuguese man-of-wars *(Physalia)* that are its favorite food, comes into the surf along the southeast coast of Florida and is glimpsed by startled surfers. The 1-inch spiral, internal shells of the deep-seasquid *Spirula spirula* are cast ashore on the Atlantic beach from Cape Cod southward, representing a 3-inch animal that normally lives between the 600- and 3,000-foot level in the open ocean. Once in a great while, the rotting carcass of a giant squid *(Architeuthis)* is left by the cold waves on the shores of Newfoundland. A few specimens have confirmed estimates that some species attain a body length of 15 feet, a diameter of 5 feet, and an overall dimension close to 60 feet, making them the largest known invertebrates. The suckers on the long tentacles of these monsters sometimes leave scars 9 inches across on the skin around the mouth of sperm whales, which pursue and eat *Architeuthis* despite the great underwater battles that this entails.

The Peanut Worms *(Phylum Sipunculoidea)*

When a peanut worm pulls in the slender anterior half or third of its cylindrical, unsegmented body it resembles the edible seed of a peanut; otherwise, the forward portion runs smoothly in and out while mucus-covered tentacles at the tip sweep up microscopic plants and other bits of nourishment from the sea

Peanut Worm (Golfingia agassizi)
Echiuroid female (Bonellia viridis)

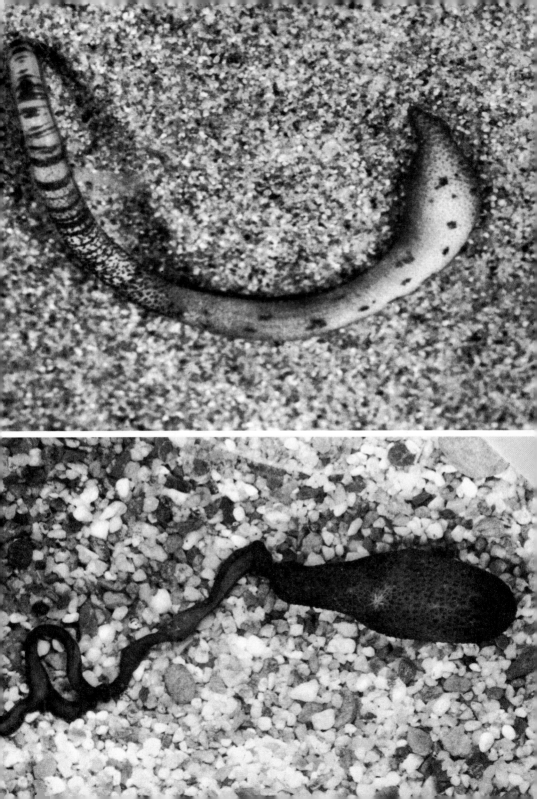

floor. The food is digested in a long intestine which is both looped upon itself to open at an anus well forward on the ventral surface and also spirally twisted.

Sipunculus nudus, which attains a length of about 8 inches and a diameter of 1/2 inch, is almost cosmopolitan in sandy shallows. *Golfingia (Phascolosoma) gouldi* burrows in mud and sandy mud near the low-tide line in southern New England, where it sometimes stretches to a length of 18 inches. The smaller *P. margaritacea* lives at greater depths along northern shores of America on both coasts. Well south along the California coast, *Dendrostoma zostericolum* lives in sand among the matted roots of surfgrass, while another species *(D. petraeus)* is often abundant beneath rocks.

The Echiuroids *(Phylum Echiuroidea)*

The approximately 150 kinds of marine worms placed in this phylum begin life as swimming larvae. In their development, they subdivide the body into exactly 15 segments—and then lose all evidence of segmentation. They mature to a general sausage shape, with a nonretractible proboscis that is troughlike or spoonshaped and ciliated on its concave surface.

Echiurus echiurus, which grows to a length of 12 inches in shallow Atlantic waters from Long Island to Greenland and the English Channel and around coasts of the North Pacific, extends its 4-inch proboscis from its burrow opening and sweeps up organic matter from the sea floor. If a fish seizes the proboscis, the worm amputates the member and quickly grows a new one. *Urechis caupo*, of the intertidal zone from California to Chile, remains concealed while pumping a current of water through its U-shaped burrow. Food particles as small as 1/6,000,000 inch are captured in a thimble-shaped mucous net which is secreted by the prostomium and swallowed when loaded. Commensal animals of several kinds live in the same burrows with *Urechis*.

The Priapulids *(Phylum Priapulida)*

The eight different kinds of marine worms that constitute this little phylum are found burrowing in mud or sand, or slowly moving their cylindrical bodies

Priapulid Worm (Priapulus caudatus)

through rock crevices and shell debris on the bottom. Locomotion is achieved mostly by activity of a barrel-shaped proboscis region, which is armed with lengthwise rows of spines and warts on a heavy cuticle. The unsegmented trunk is more flexible because on it the similar cuticle falls into between 30 and 100 ringlike folds on which the spines are smaller and less regular. The cuticle over the entire body is molted and replaced several times a year. One or two large, soft, gill-like outgrowths arise posteriorly, close to the anus.

Larval priapulids resemble rotifers and apparently eat algal cells and organic detritus. The adults prey upon slow-moving invertebrates with soft bodies, such as some polychaete worms. North American priapulids, from 1 to 6 inches in length, are known from a depth of 6 feet below low-tide line to at least 1,500 feet, chiefly from Boston harbor northward on the Atlantic coast and from Tomales Bay, California, to the Arctic in Pacific waters. *Priapulus caudatus,* with a long proboscis, is ivory-colored or brown, whereas *Halicryptus spinulosus*, with a short proboscis, is usually pink. At least in *Priapulus*, the fluid in the body cavity contains cells bearing the red pigment hemerythrin.

Until 1951, the priapulids were grouped with the peanut worms (Sipunculoidea) and the echiuroids as strange, unsegmented members of a special class (the Gephyrea) of Phylum Annelida. Then an apparent lack of any peritoneum around the body cavity in priapulids led to their inclusion among the Aschelminthes, while the peanut worms and echiuroids were accorded separate phylum rank. Research by W. L. Shapeero published in 1961 showed, however, that a thin membrane that surrounds the priapulid body cavity is actually cellular and a peritoneum, although the nuclei are so small as to be invisible except through the electron microscope. On this basis the priapulids are again included among the coelomates and given a phylum of their own.

The Segmented Worms
(Phylum Annelida)

Marine worms have been leaving trails behind them in the surface of the ocean bottom since Pre-Cambrian times. But not until the middle of the Cambrian period, perhaps 550 million years ago, did any of these soft-bodied animals leave an identifiable fossil that showed the repetition of body parts, segment after segment, characteristic of the members of this phylum. If in no other way, the subdivision of the body internally into a series of similar units, known as segments, is made evident externally by ringlike grooves that correspond to the position of the crosswise partitions, called septa. This conspicuous feature gives the phylum its name, taken from a French corruption of the Latin *anellis*, a ring.

In many annelid worms, the segments nearest the mouth are conspicuously specialized for feeding and often for respiration as well. The most posterior segment, which bears the anus, may be extended into two or more sensory projections. But the segments between head and tail are generally much alike, each containing one ganglion and local innervation from the lengthwise nerve cord, a local set of blood vessels connected to the common lengthwise trunks, a portion of the lengthwise tubular digestive tract, and a pair of excretory tubules (nephridia) that discharge wastes from the body cavity.

With specific variations, this basic pattern suffices for about 8,500 different kinds of worms as they meet the challenges of their environment. More than 5,000 species swim or burrow in marine habitats, scavenging in the bottom muds down to the deepest abysses or performing amazing mating ballets in surface waters. About 3,000 kinds live in fresh waters, or till the soil as earthworms. A minority—less than 300 species—are predatory and parasitic leeches. Together, the segmented worms are an important part of the diet of many coelenterates, flatworms, nemerteans, other annelid worms, crustaceans, and insects, sea stars and serpent stars, fishes, and terrestrial vertebrates. A "fishworm" is almost always an annelid.

The Paddle-footed Annelids (Class Polychaeta)

Often the thin vanelike paddles that extend laterally, one pair per segment, or the soft elongated finger-like or threadlike projections that collect food or oxygen for marine annelids are more conspicuous than the multiple bristles for which the class is named. Actually, the bristles support the vanes (parapodia) with which a polychaete worm swims and which greatly enlarge the vascular surface through which it carries on respiratory exchange of gases. The inner ends of the bristles are under muscular control, which enables the worm to wave its parapodia in a rhythmic and effective fashion, whether in swimming or in creating a current of water through its burrow.

Coastal fishermen seek out clamworms, chiefly *Nereis*, as ideal bait, because these animals are well adjusted to salt water and will continue to wriggle for an hour or more while impaled on a hook. Nereids may bite for they have a pair of horny teeth embedded in the muscular wall of the pharynx portion of their digestive tract. A worm that is trying to defend itself, or pull itself along out of water, or capture and engulf some food, turns its throat region inside out through its open mouth. This exposes the teeth and separates them widely. When the nereid pulls in its pharynx, the jaws close on whatever they can seize. When continued, this retraction can pull a small victim deep inside the worm's body.

Some kinds of nereids are as big as small snakes. *Nereis (Neanthes) virens* attains a length of 18 inches along New England shores, particularly where the bottom near low-tide mark is muddy sand; this species is also found in cool waters on both sides of the North Atlantic and along the Pacific coast of North America. Its body is always a handsome reddish brown, glistening with a greenish iridescent sheen. Pacific shores have also *N. brandti*, which can become

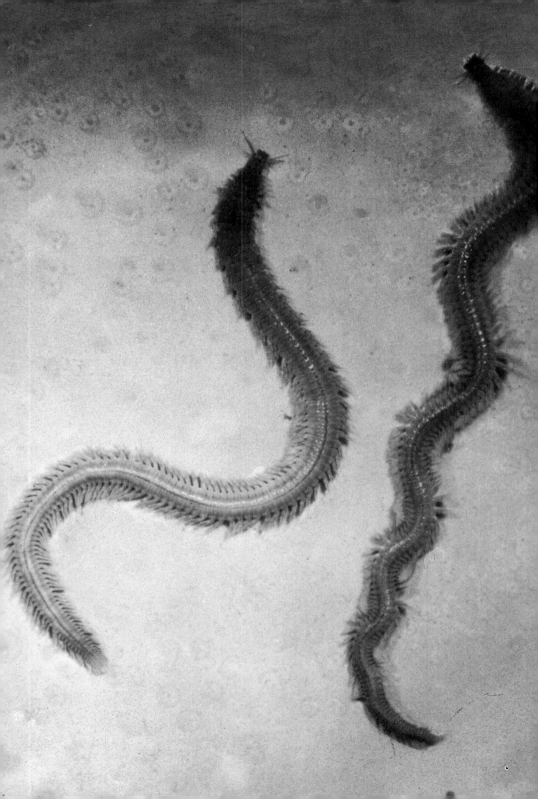

as broad as a garter snake and fully 36 inches long. But many other species are less than an inch in length. Characteristically, they swarm to the surface of the sea at a specific time of year, of a lunar month, and of a day (or a night) to reproduce. Either the whole individual participates, or it amputates its hinder half as a "heteronereis"—a reproductive portion that is self-propelled, expendable, and replaceable through regeneration. Whichever arrives at the surface, the female components of the mating population appear stiff and inflexible, driving themselves along by movements only of their paddles; virtually every segment is tightly packed with eggs. The male components, by contrast, swim in dizzy spirals at much greater speed. Eventually, a male spirals his way along the length of a female's body. She responds to this stimulation by exploding, pouring eggs into the water through rents in her body wall. The male reacts immediately, also bursting, and freeing his sperms among her eggs. Fertilization is external, and the reproducing parents die, sinking to the bottom.

The fundamental differences among polychaetes are in chemical details, sensitivity, and behavior. Yet to know one kind of worm from another, structural features are more useful. Members of genus *Glycera* have four, rather than two, pharyngeal teeth. Species of *Eunice* and *Diopatra* possess a more complex jaw apparatus. Even more helpful in telling worms apart are varying degrees of development in the parts of the parapodia and of sensory structures on the head. Indeed, such features as aciculae, cirri, palps, parapodia and tentacles have stimulated scientists who specialize in worms to name many after girls or the graceful nereids with which Greek mythmakers peopled the seas: for example, *Amphitrite, Aphrodite, Eunice*, and *Ophelia*.

Commonly, the slender swimming worms, *Autolytus, Syllis* and *Odontosyllis*, are called syllids, because their bodies resemble somewhat a string of beads and the Greek *psellion* signifies a necklace. *Autolytus* adds new segments to its string, and then breaks into fragments, each a new individual that can repeat the asexual process of reproduction. *Odontosyllis* has become famous as "the fireworm," because its luminescent swarmers come to the surface of the sea at night in such numbers that the waters become bright with their cold light. The 1/2-inch *O. fulgurans*, with as many as 64 segments, is common on pilings and under stones near shore along the Atlantic coast; it often provides a nocturnal display in summer. A related species, *O. enopla*, which inhabits warmer waters close to Bermuda and various islands in the Bahamas and West Indies, has been credited with producing the mysterious lights that were recorded in the logbook of Christopher Columbus on October 11, 1492.

Related worms with more compact bodies creep about decorously upon the sea floor, scavenging for organic matter of many kinds. Largest of them is the sea mouse *(Aphrodite aculeata)*, whose 7-inch, humped body may be 1 inch high and 3 inches wide. Under a dense felt of long grayish hairs along its back and green-to-gold iridescent hairs along its flanks are 15 pairs of hard, over-lapping scales. Other and more common scale worms lack hairs. *Harmothoe*, with 15 pairs of scales, and *Lepidonotus*, with 12 pairs, grow to from 1 to 3 inches long and are often found hiding under stones in tide pools along most coasts.

Paddle-footed annelids that move about freely are referred to as members of the "Errantia" to distinguish them from very similar worms whose specializa-tions fit them for life in tubes of their own construction or in burrows that they make and maintain in the sea floor. Among the most conspicuous of these contrasting members of the "Sedentaria" are the plumed worms *(Diopatra cupraea)* of the Atlantic coast from New England to Brazil. They reinforce and camouflage a projecting 2- to 4-inch chimney above their vertical tubular burrow by cementing to the secreted lining assorted bits of seaweed and shell that are captured while the tide is in. The animal itself holds its plumed head out of its doorway.

The parchment-tube worm is *Chaetopterus variopedatus*, which produces a U-shaped burrow in muddy sand of the sea floor close to the low-tide mark, and lines the cavity with secreted material. Never exposing itself or adding any other reinforcement, the worm lies at the bottom of its tube, pumping water past its body and filtering out the microorganisms by means of a thimble-shaped net of mucus. A specialized pair of parapodia secrete this net and hold it in place except when, at 15- to 20-minute intervals, the worm stops pumping, rolls its mucus net into a ball and swallows it. For no known reason, *Chaetopterus* is luminous at night. Glowing from the 6-inch worm, the light may show at both ends of the 15-inch tube.

Flowerlike displays of slender, colorful tentacles often attract attention to tube-dwelling annelids whose bodies are well concealed. These respiratory and feeding organs on the fringed worm *(Cirratulus)* are in paired clusters on the eighth and ninth segments of the 6-inch body; the clustered filaments, each with a lengthwise red blood vessel along its golden-yellow surface, extend from the front doorway of the soft tube that the worm constructs in the muddy bottom. More flowerlike is *Amphitrite*, on the head of which are three pairs of blood-red branching gills and a large number of flesh-colored tentacles, dis-played from the doorway of a tube reinforced with grains of sand among stones and on pilings. The feather-duster worms (such as *Sabella*) bear two tufts of long plumelike breathing organs, which are withdrawn at the slightest commotion into the leathery or parchment-like tube, which may be 15 inches long. By contrast, the tiny serpulids (such as *Spirorbis* in shallow coastal waters) generally attach their stiff limy tubes to some firm support. *Spirorbis* is often mistaken for a snail shell 1/4 inch across, attached by one side to a seaweed; the illusion is enhanced when the worm retracts its body, for then it uses a modified tentacle as a plug for the aperture of its flat spiral tube.

Some polychaetes of considerable size get along with no special tube or reinforcement. Along both coasts of America, the lugworm *(Arenicola)* uses its eversible, toothless pharynx as a burrowing tool, and as it works its way through the bottom mud swallows the mud in lumps at approximately 5-second intervals. From time to time, the worm extends its posterior end to the end of its U-shaped burrow and adds to the neat coils of castings there. These castings accumulate and erode into miniature volcanoes on the bottom. The worm itself is seldom seen, although its body may be more than 15 inches long and over an inch in diameter. When caught, *Arenicola* seems too limp and inert to use for fish bait. Extra encircling wrinkles conceal the fact that the trunk part of the body has only about 21 segments. This region bears bristles, and also tufts of bright red gills.

The Bristle-footed Annelids (Class Oligochaeta)

An earthworm of land or of fresh water is different from a lugworm (or other polychaete) in more ways than just an intolerance for salt water, a lack of gills and of parapodia. Ordinarily, the sexes are combined in a hermaphroditic individual, rather than separated as among polychaetes, and the sex organs are permanent, discharging through special ducts, rather than temporary and ridding the worm of eggs or sperm by rupture. The parapodia are represented in an oligochaete (the word comes from the Greek *oligo*, meaning few, and *chaeta*, meaning bristles) by four pairs of bristles per segment, all under muscular control.

Oligochaetes tend to be worldwide in distribution, particularly those that inhabit fresh water. Little *Dero*, barely 1/4 inch long, secretes a slender tube below a duckweed leaf and darts part way out of either door to capture small crustaceans such as water fleas that pause below the floating plant. Inch-long *Tubifex* benefit from organic materials on the bottom of deep lakes and polluted streams, where oxygen is virtually lacking, by being able to breathe anaerobically and remain almost free of predators while feeding on the detritus. Each worm holds to its blind, mucus-lined burrow in the bottom while digging in for food. The posterior end usually projects and waves, producing a current that aids in feeding. But if anything disturbs a population of *Tubifex*, the worms vanish into their tubes.

Earthworms with much the same type of body but of a larger size constitute about half of the entire weight of animal life in most soils. Each worm seeks out decaying roots and other organic foods underground, and also reaches from its doorways at night for fallen leaves and small soft fruits that it can drag into its tunnels and devour at leisure. The unwary worm that exposes itself by day is the one the robin catches.

In North America, the common earthworms are all introduced species from Europe. Fishermen prefer the large "night crawler" *(Lumbricus terrestris)*, which grows nearly a foot long and has a flattened tail, to the 3-inch *Allolobophora caliginosa* that is the commonest earthworm in America, or to the brandling *(Eisenia foetida)* of similar size, which is easy to dig out of manure piles, compost heaps and decaying stumps. *Eisenia* can be distinguished from a young *Lumbricus* because its body has only about 95 (not 150) segments, and bears the glandular swollen clitellum between segments 25 and 32 (not 32 to 37, as in *Lumbricus*). Contrary to popular belief, these worms can regenerate only the first 2 or 3 segments and those following the 40th. If cut in two between segments 3 and 40, both "halves" of the worm die. A worm that loses all of its body following segment 40 can restore one surviving worm. It replaces first the terminal segment, containing a new anus. Then this segment regenerates new intervening segments until the total in the worm is the same, within about one per cent, as the worm had when it first emerged into the world as a 1-inch youngster.

The Leeches (Class Hirudinea)

A hungry leech is so wrinkled transversely that it shows no indication of having only about 34 segments in its body. Internally, its body cavity is almost obliterated by connective tissue and strong muscles that serve in body movements, in operating the one or two powerful suckers and perhaps three sharp jaws with which it can slice through vertebrate skin or cut up small animals as food. Most leeches live in fresh water, but a few kinds lurk in marine situations where they

Sabellid Feather-duster Worm (*Eudistylia polymorpha*)
150

can prey on fish, and still fewer inhabit humid tropical lands, where they attach themselves to terrestrial vertebrates and suck huge meals of blood.

The best known leech is the Eurasian *Hirudo medicinalis*, a pond-dweller that tolerates handling and culture as a domestic animal. For many years it has been used in primitive medicine to suck out "bad blood," and more recently to remove the color from a black eye. When hungry, it will attach itself where placed on human skin and use its potent saliva to liquefy a blood clot beneath the skin. This same anticoagulant prevents a blood meal from solidifying inside the crop of the leech. A full-grown medicinal leech may expand from a length of 6 inches to as much as 12, and need no more than one big meal a month.

The American horse leech *(Haemopis marmorata)*, about 4 inches long, lives in streams, ditches, and pool edges, feeding on aquatic worms and mollusks between opportunities to suck blood from wading birds and mammals. In the same situations, the turtle leech *(Placobdella parasitica)* is more likely to wait for a painted turtle or a snapping turtle, and cling at the base of the reptile's hind legs. All of these leeches remain flattened out until they have become engorged with blood. The common brook leech or "worm leech" *(Herpobdella punctata)* is more cylindrical, and differs from the others in lacking jaws. This seems no handicap, for a *Herpobdella* can swallow smaller worms and insect larvae whole, or live for weeks on decaying organic matter, or cling most tenaciously while getting a blood meal.

In the marine world, leeches of the genus *Branchellion* seem to prefer feeding on skates and rays, whereas those of *Piscicola* attack bony fishes. *Branchellion* has a huge posterior sucker and small leaflike lobed gills along the sides of its flattened body. *Piscicola* is cylindrical, long and slender until engorged, and particularly numerous on the upper side of the summer flounder *(Pseudopleuronectes)* along the New England coast.

The Arthropods *(Phylum Arthropoda)*

In the immense variety of animals on earth, seven out of every ten kinds are insects. Yet the insects constitute only part of the great phylum whose members secrete a skeletal support external to their skin, and move their paired appendages —legs or some equivalent—at definite hinge joints in that external skeleton. The jointed legs give the arthropods their phylum name, from the Greek *arthron*,

Night Crawler (Lumbricus terrestris)

meaning a joint. It is a feature found in about 88,000 kinds of animals that are arthropods but *not* insects. The variety among non-insect arthropods is about the same as in the second and third largest phyla combined: the mollusks, with about 45,000 species and the chordates, with some 43,000 (most of which are vertebrates).

The natural subdivisions among living arthropods include two minor subphyla and two major ones. The bear animalcules (subphylum and class Tardigrada) number only about 350 different species. The peculiar, parasitic tongue worms (subphylum and class Pentastomida) are less than a fifth as numerous in kinds. The most successful category, if variety is equated with success, are the arthropods with paired jaws (subphylum Mandibulata), which include the crustaceans, centipedes, millipedes and lesser kin as well as all the insects. The runners-up are the arthropods with leglike chelicerae instead of jaws (subphylum Chelicerata), which include the horseshoe crabs and sea spiders in marine habitats, and the scorpions, land spiders, and mites in terrestrial and freshwater environments.

The Bear Animalcules (Class Tardigrada)

The biggest bear animalcule is only about 1/30 inch long. When most active, it marches along slowly on four pairs of legs, three pairs arising from the sides of its stout body and a final pair at the posterior end. Each leg ends in a little cluster of 4 or 5 sharp claws or hooks that are movable and also helpful in clinging to a moss plant, a lichen, a bit of bark, or a shingle on a roof. While its environment is wet, or at least very humid, the little animal prowls for prey or scavenges for food, sucking microscopic organic matter into its small mouth or cutting it free with a pair of needle-like teeth. But at the first sign of dry weather, the tardigrade loses water, becomes shriveled and dormant. It can then be blown about as a dust particle, which explains why most kinds of bear animalcules are cosmopolitan. They can remain dormant for years, tolerate indefinitely temperatures as low as liquid air, and then become active again in a few hours when wet or exposed to very humid air at the right temperature. Tardigrades of a dozen different genera are known, some from marine environments, some from terrestrial, and most from fresh waters.

The Tongue Worms (Class Pentastomida)

These soft, wormlike parasites reach vertebrate animals in uncooked meat, are freed in the stomach or small intestine, and make their way as larvae to the nasal cavities and lungs where they mature. Each adult has a body 3/4 to 5 inches long, in which a cephalothorax region can be distinguished from a flexible, ringed (but unsegmented) abdomen. Two pairs of ventral hooks near the mouth hold the parasite in place, but let it reach about for a mate. Females lay eggs that pass into the gut and out with the feces. Usually a different animal is needed by the hatchling larva as the place in which to grow, molt after molt, and then wait until its new host is eaten by the vertebrate predator or scavenger in which the tongue worm can mature. Larval tongue worms, which have 4 to 6 leglike appendages (each with sharp, movable claws), have been found in almost every class of vertebrate animal that could serve as food for a reptile,

153

bird, or mammal. Rabbits seem to be the principal intermediate hosts for *Linguatula*, which reaches maturity in canines such as wolves and dogs.

The Crustaceans (Class Crustacea)

The two pairs of antennae, one pair of jaws, and two pairs of mouthparts, known as maxillae, are more distinctive features of crustaceans than any other in the body. Often the head of the animal is joined broadly to the trunk region, forming a cephalothorax. Ordinarily the abdomen shows its fundamental segmented character. It and the thorax region generally bear a series of paired appendages, each of which is basically forked. But variations on this underlying theme are so numerous that different crustaceans are well adapted for life among the drifting plankton, swimming in the deep dark midwaters of the ocean, creeping over the ocean floor, burrowing in the bottom, attacking other animals as parasites, inhabiting fresh waters, and adopting a terrestrial existence, at least as adults. During their lifetime, many crustaceans move from one habitat to another. Yet so great a preponderance of species are marine that the members of this class have been called the "insects of the sea."

Members of more than 30 orders of crustaceans can be found in North America. To keep so many in a comprehensible array, the malacologists who study crustaceans have grouped their subjects into eight subclasses: (1) The Cephalocarida, with one order and four species, all 1/8-inch, slender, blind, shrimplike creatures discovered since 1954, living in the bottom sand and mud of Long Island Sound *(Hutchinsoniella macracantha)*, San Francisco Bay *(Lightiella serendipita)*, the West Indies and Japan; (2) the Branchiopoda or "phyllopods," which include the brine shrimps and fairy shrimps (order Anostraca), the tadpole shrimps (Notostraca), the clam shrimps (Conchostraca), and the water fleas (Cladocera); (3) the Ostracoda, including four orders of seed shrimps; (4) the Mystacocarida, with one order and 3 species of *Derocheilocarus*, each about 1/50 inch long and adapted to life between the sand grains of beaches as far apart as New England and South Africa; (5) the Copepoda, with seven orders that include important members of the plankton community in marine and freshwater situations and also some extraordinarily degenerate parasites; (6) the Branchiura, with one order and about 75 species of external parasites known as fish lice; (7) the Cirripedia, including several orders of barnacles; and (8) the Malacostraca, with 10 orders and more than 18,000 species including the shrimps and prawns, lobsters and crayfishes, crabs and beach fleas, freshwater scuds and terrestrial sow bugs. To become intimately acquainted with so many would take several lifetimes. But a few representatives do catch the attention of those attuned to the outdoor world.

THE PHYLLOPODS *(Subclass Branchiopoda)*

"Instant shrimp," as sold in pet stores, are the amazingly resistant eggs of 1/3-inch brine shrimps *(Artemia salina)*. The eggs sometimes accumulate in layers 2 to 3 inches thick around the shores of Great Salt Lake, in Utah. When immersed in salt water of the right concentration, the eggs hatch into young crustaceans that can tolerate salinities from fresh water to saturated brine. They are excellent food for aquarium fishes if they do not contain excessive concentrations of DDT from agricultural fields that drain into the salt lakes. *Artemia* lives on salt-tolerant microscopic algae and swims about inverted to gather this nourishment. Rhythmic waving of feathery feet propels the crustacean while its leg bases filter out and manipulate the algae ready for swallowing. Essentially, the same habit is followed in temporary ponds early each spring by fairy shrimps *(Eubranchipus vernalis)*, which mature to a length of about 1 inch and swim about inverted in mated, tandem pairs. The eggs that are dropped remain dormant for almost a year, then magically give rise to another generation. The tadpole shrimps, *Triops* and *Lepidurus*, which have a shield-shaped covering over the cephalothorax and attain a length of more than 1 inch, appear with similar suddenness in western states and provinces when dry lake beds are turned into shallow ponds by local heavy rain, perhaps after years with only caked mud to mark the site. Birds may arrive to feast on phyllopods, but no predatory fishes can wait so long between one filling of the pond and the next.

Clam shrimps and water fleas live in more permanent bodies of fresh water and thereby have an important role in converting planktonic algae into food that fishes eat. Clam shrimps typically are seen in late spring and summer months, in warmer water than most other phyllopods; *Lynceus* and *Cyzicus* are most numerous in the southern and western United States, where each individual glides along without obvious means of propulsion because its short legs do not extend beyond its bivalved carapace. Water fleas, by contrast, twitch in their locomotion, which is accomplished by movements of the elongated antennae. The largest of them, *Leptodora kindtii*, which attains a length of 3/4 inch in lakes of the northern United States and Canada, lays winter eggs and goes through a larval (nauplius) stage. All other cladocerans develop directly from either fertilized (winter) eggs or parthenogenetic brood; they tend to be cosmo-politan, apparently because their winter eggs can stand being dried in mud on the feet of a migrating bird and also survive passage through the bird's digestive tract. Best known is *Daphnia*, a creature first described in 1699 by the Dutch microscopist Jan Swammerdam as *Pulex aquaticus arborescens*—the water flea with branching arms. A *Daphnia* 1/8 inch long produces a new brood of young every two or three days, all of them females and soon able to reproduce on their own; males appear only late in the summer. A few water fleas, such as *Evadne* and *Podon*, reproduce in the saline environment of saltmarshes and estuaries, particularly along the Atlantic coast.

THE OSTRACODS (Subclass Ostracoda)

Although concealed in a bivalved shell that makes it resemble a clam shrimp, an ostracod can generally be recognized by its jerky mode of progression through the water or over the bottom detritus on which it feeds. This is because it moves its seed-shaped body entirely by means of the projecting tips of its antennae. Few ostracods are more than 1/8 inch long. About a third of the 1,800 species live in fresh water, and the remainder in marine shallows. *Cypris* is a common genus in ponds and marshes, and unusual among ostracods in reproducing parthenogenetically. The marine genera *Cypridina* and *Conchoecia* contain many luminous species.

THE COPEPODS (Subclass Copepoda)

Between May and November, almost every pond in temperate North America contains thousands of copepods swimming about. Each one has a pear-shaped body, mostly less than 1/8 inch long, and progresses blunt end foremost in jerky fashion as the little animal rows with its several pairs of thoracic legs. The Greek *kope* signifies an oar. While progressing in this fashion, the long second antennae are folded back along the sides. When the copepod rests, it spreads its antennae to the sides, which helps keep it from sinking in the water.

The commonest copepods in fresh water are species of *Cyclops* not over 1/16 inch long, yet named for the one-eyed giant of Greek mythology. Females carry their eggs with them in two huge masses, one on each side of the tapering abdomen. Like most copepod eggs, these hatch as one-eyed larvae with three pairs of swimming appendages: the first and second pairs of antennae, and the elongated, fringed mandibles. After several molts, this "nauplius" stage trans-forms to the adult style of body.

Marine copepods may be exceedingly numerous in surface waters at night and scarce there during the day. Even in the open sea they tend to migrate into dark depths, starting down before sunrise and returning to feed at the surface at dusk. *Calanus finmarchicus*, which is about the size of a big grain of rice, travels at a speed of about 150 feet per hour between its feeding zone in the topmost 150 feet of water and its daytime hideaway 1,100 to 1,500 feet below the surface. The gain from so much travel seems to be in riding deep currents in one direction all day and surface currents in another direction at night. This brings the copepod into a new feeding territory as it approaches the surface. Along with the copepods in this up-and-down travel go many arrow worms, small fishes, and other animals that eat copepods, plus a considerable assortment of larger fishes and squids that prey upon the copepod-eaters.

Of the three orders of copepods that are free-living, the calanoids (order Calanoida) are largely planktonic, such as *Calanus* in the sea and *Diaptomus* in fresh water and some saline lakes. The harpacticoids (Harpacticoida) tend to associate with the bottom detritus in coastal waters, and in brackish and fresh waters. The cyclopoids (Cyclopoida), such as *Cyclops* in fresh water and *Oithona* in marine shallows, include both planktonic and bottom-dwelling kinds.

Of the many crustaceans that have evolved parasitic habits, most are copepods. In a few instances, a calanoid species has varied from the free-living habit with little modification, in that the female attaches herself by hooked antennae to the gills of a fish and takes her nourishment from its blood stream; *Ergasilus versicolor* is often found on the gill filaments of freshwater fishes. But more than a thousand species in four whole orders of copepods have become exclusively parasitic, either as larvae inside polychaete worms, or as adults inside the pharynx of a tunicate, or as a mature female (at least) attached externally to some fish in the marine environment or fresh water. Her body may degenerate into a formless bag, but she still produces two sacs full of eggs reminiscent of those in *Cyclops*. In some instances the adult males are parasitic too. More often they are free-swimming, and so are the larvae of parasitic adults.

THE BRANCHIURANS (Subclass Branchiura)

The most conspicuous fish lice are members of the genus *Argulus*, in which the body is covered by a flat oval or circular carapace as much as 1 inch across. Embedded in its surface are two compound eyes quite unlike those of any copepod. The first pair of maxillae are modified into suction cups, with which *Argulus* holds to the skin or the mouth lining of a fish while sucking blood. Again,

Overleaf: top left, Female Copepod (Cyclops) with paired egg masses; bottom left, Brine Shrimp (Artemia salina); top right, Water Flea (Simocephalus) with four winter eggs; bottom right, Ostracod

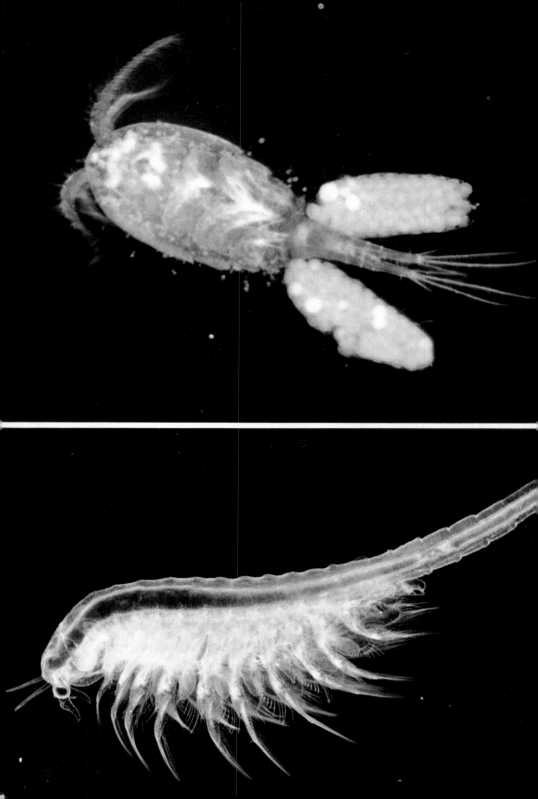

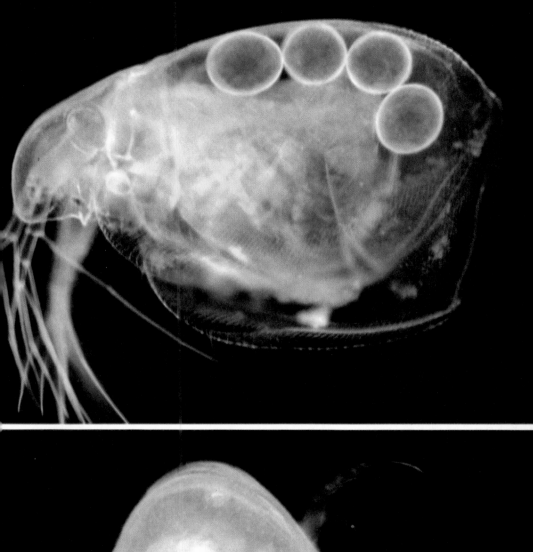
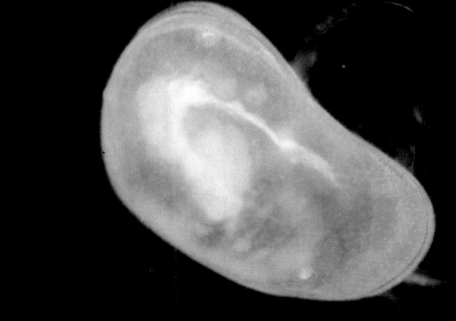

unlike any parasitic copepod, *Argulus* is ready at any time to leave its victim and swim to another. But the name of the subclass and order (signifying gills on the tail) perpetuate a mistake: *Argulus* has respiratory areas under its carapace but no gills at all.

THE BARNACLES *(Subclass Cirripedia)*

The right of a barnacle to a place among the crustaceans is shown by its larval stages. The youngest is a nauplius, which transforms into a bivalved form so like the ostracod *Cypris* that it is called a "cyprid" stage. The cyprid attaches itself to some firm support by means of the first pair of head appendages, called antennules. For a short time, the young barnacle ceases to feed while its body undergoes a transformation. The little animal absorbs or discards its eyes, obliterates its abdomen, and reduces its paired appendages to six or four feathery feet called cirri, from which the order Cirripedia gets its name. Around its body the barnacle secretes a limy shell composed of 5 or 6 interlocking plates, plus a movable 4-piece door that can be opened and shut quickly. Through the opened door the animal reaches out with its feet and captures particles of food. The first monographic account of this group of animals was a two-volume work by Charles Darwin in 1851. It established his reputation as a professional zoologist eight years before publication of *The Origin of Species*.

Barnacles are all marine, fastening themselves for the most part on rocks near the intertidal zone. Rocks, wharf pilings, and ship bottoms are commonly covered by a rough coating of sessile acorn barnacles *(Balanus* and *Chthamalus)* or support lively clusters of gooseneck barnacles *(Lepas)* each of which bears its armored body atop a flexible, leathery stalk. The barnacles on ship bottoms are "fouling organisms" because they greatly increase the frictional drag of the hull upon the water. Many ways have been tried to make the hull unattractive to the cyprid stage, so that barnacles would not attach themselves in the first place. Removing them later by scraping the hull, with the ship idle in dry dock, is expensive and laborious.

The skin of whales attracts barnacle cyprids, principally those of *Coronula,* an acorn barnacle as much as 3 inches in diameter. The shell of *Coronula,* in turn, becomes the attachment surface for the gooseneck barnacle *Conchoderma,* which has only a minimal shell and keeps its feeding organs protected in little hoods that open in the direction toward which the whale swims. The paired hoods on *Conchoderma* have inspired the name rabbit-eared barnacle for this cirripede.

Intertidal Goose Barnacles (Pollicipes polymerus)
and Bay Mussels (Mytilus edulis)

A number of barnacles have become parasitic, "root-headed" organisms that show spectacular degeneration. Best known of them is *Sacculina*, which attacks various kinds of crabs along both coasts of America. The larva of this barnacle enters its host through a hollow bristle, and floats about in the blood until it reaches a point between the crab's stomach and intestine. There the parasite attaches itself, absorbing nourishment from the blood and extending a mass of rootlike processes throughout the crab's body. The *Sacculina* destroys the reproductive organs of the host, and this alters the hormonal balance in the crab, causing the animal to assume the female form of body at the next molt, regardless of its inherited sex. Female body form includes a wide, apron-like abdomen; this shields *Sacculina* when it creates an opening in the crab's body wall and extrudes a large shapeless mass. Within the mass, eggs develop parthenogenetically to the nauplius stage, before escaping to infect and sterilize more crabs.

THE MALACOSTRACANS (Subclass Malacostraca)

The majority, as well as the largest, of crustaceans, the most powerful, and many of the small weak kinds are grouped into this subclass because of their body structure. The head region is fused to one or more thoracic segments and the six segments of the abdomen are usually freely movable. Commonly, the head and thorax are armored above by a carapace and the abdomen bears paired appendages. Six of the 10 orders are well represented in North America.

The Opossum Shrimps (Order Mysidacea)

Most of the 450 species in this little order live in the dark depths of the sea, where they grow to lengths mostly between 1/2 and 2 inches; a few exceptional species are 30 inches long. All of these animals have a pair of big compound eyes on movable stalks, many feathery feet below both a short cephalothorax region with a carapace and additional separate thoracic segments, and a slender cylindrical abdomen. Several species of *Mysis*, 1-1/4 inches long, can be found in tide pools or hiding among seaweed. *M. stenolepis*, which is abundant in coastal and intertidal waters from New Jersey to the Gulf of St. Lawrence, forms an important item in the diet of shad and small flounders. *M. oculata*, characteristic of cold northern waters, appears to have been trapped during the Ice Ages and evolved a separate subspecies, *M. o. relicta*, adapted to fresh water, which inhabits the Great Lakes and some of the Finger Lakes in New York State, and is a major source of food for lake trout. On the Pacific coast, *Neomysis*

Preceding page: top left, Freshwater Isopod (Asellus sp.); bottom left, Wharf Bug (Idotea sp.); right, Goose Barnacle (Lepas fascicularis)

Cosmopolitan pillbug (Armadillidium vulgare)

mercedis is common in brackish water and even invades some rivers and strictly freshwater lakes.

The Isopods (Order Isopoda)

Although most of the 4,000 different kinds of crustaceans in this order are marine, the freshwater and land species are more familiar. The name of the order refers to the 7 pairs of similar legs that extend to the sides from below a corresponding number of separate thoracic segments; there is no carapace. Below the short abdomen are inconspicuous flattened appendages used in respiration. Typically, the free-living isopods and those that are external parasites on fishes have a broad, mildly convex body. Species that are internal parasites of fishes show degenerative changes as they mature.

The most active and alert of isopods has become almost ubiquitous on and around wharfs on temperate sea coasts: it is the wharf bug *(Idotea baltica)*, of which males are less than 1/2 inch long but females often 1-1/2. Both sexes tend to be dark green and to slither into crevices as though they were cockroaches. A smaller relative, the 1/5-inch gribble *(Limnoria lignorum)* is essentially cosmo-

Overleaf: Skeleton Shrimps (Caprella sp.)

politan, but is less often seen because it usually remains below the water level, excavating cavities 1/2 inch deep into timbers and wooden hulls, causing their eventual destruction.

Members of the genus *Asellus*, mostly less than 1 inch long, are common in fresh and stagnant water on muddy bottoms, eating organic matter where few other animals are found. Females carry below the anterior 5 pairs of legs a brood pouch that is generally full of eggs or young all summer, with a new brood every six weeks or so.

The terrestrial isopods nourish themselves on fungi and decaying organic matter, hiding under stones, fallen logs, in crevices of the soil, and damp basements. Known as sow bugs, woodlice or slaters, they are sometimes called "pill bugs," although this name should be reserved for those that can roll the body into an almost perfect sphere and stay curled for a minute or more after being disturbed. This behavior is shown by the cosmopolitan black *Armadillidium vulgare* and the shiny, earth-brown *Cylisticus convexus*, which has been introduced from Europe into the eastern United States. Others in the same 1/2-inch size range and gray to brown hue, and able only to fold themselves temporarily into a U-shape, include the native *Porcellio scaber*, which has a rough back, and the introduced *Oniscus asellus* of Europe, which is smooth and often shiny. Both are common across the northern United States and Canada.

The Amphipods (Order Amphipoda)

The majority of the 4,000 different species of amphipods associate themselves with the sea floor, from intertidal shallows to the greatest abysses. There they run along nimbly, their bodies slightly hump-backed and laterally compressed but with no carapace to hide the segmentation. The name of the order (Amphipoda) refers to the customary arrangement of the legs, with the anterior pairs reaching downward and forward and the posterior pairs turned backward or even upward. In shallow water, an amphipod turns on its side and kicks itself along easily. This behavior is seen most often in the 1/2-inch freshwater scuds *(Gammarus* and *Hyallela)*, which are widely distributed; *Gammarus* has species in coastal waters too. These crustaceans swim short distances, climb submerged vegetation, feed on both living and dead plant material, and are important items in the diet of fishes in shallow water.

The same body form is characteristic of the active beach fleas or sand hoppers, such as *Orchestia* and *Talorchestia*, which hide in piles of seaweed and other beach drift or in vertical burrows of their own making. During the night, these

168

crustaceans scavenge over the sand, always ready to escape from predators by quickly flexing the back and kicking with the posterior pairs of legs, leaping repeatedly into the air.

Stranger amphipods are the skeleton shrimps *(Caprella)*, whose 1/2-inch bodies consist of an elongated series of cylindrical segments from which two pairs of slender, hooked legs arise near the head and three more pairs at the rear. The skeleton shrimp clings to seaweeds, hydroids, or wharf pilings, moving slowly while stalking smaller animals, such as copepods, that it can seize with its anterior appendages. Related amphipods known as whale lice *(Paracyamus)* creep about over the skin of whales, hooking their legs into the surface or gnawing out pits in which they take shelter from the water rushing past. They are external parasites with nowhere to go if the whale becomes stranded or is caught.

The Euphausids (Order Euphausiacea)

In many parts of the world, the principal food of whalebone whales are small pelagic crustaceans known to whalers as "krill." The 90-odd species of the order Euphausiacea are even more shrimplike than mysids, because the carapace extends posteriorly and around the sides to conceal the bases of all the swimming legs. Most euphausids are brilliant red and, when numerous, color the surface waters where they feed until whalers refer to it as "tomato soup." By night, many euphausids produce their own light, and glow brightly where they are feeding or have been disturbed by a passing boat. The "night shining ones," rendered from the Greek into the generic name *Nyctiphanes*, sometimes swim so close to shore along North Atlantic coasts from Cape Cod to Greenland that they can be seen and caught from jetties. Members of *Euphausia* are seen more often among the specimens collected in nets towed behind boats farther from the shore. Along the Pacific coast, *Thysanooessa gregaria* often frequents the community of life clinging to wharf pilings just below the level of lowest tides, seemingly feeding on smaller animals that swim about in this area.

The Long-tailed Decapods (Order Decapoda)

True shrimps, lobsters, and crayfishes are easily distinguished from the crabs that, along with them, constitute the crustacean order Decapoda. The one group move along with a conspicuously segmented abdomen (the "tail") exposed behind them, whereas crabs keep an equally segmented abdomen tucked underneath where it is scarcely visible. All of these animals are named for the five

Overleaf: Commensal Shrimp on Sea Amenome

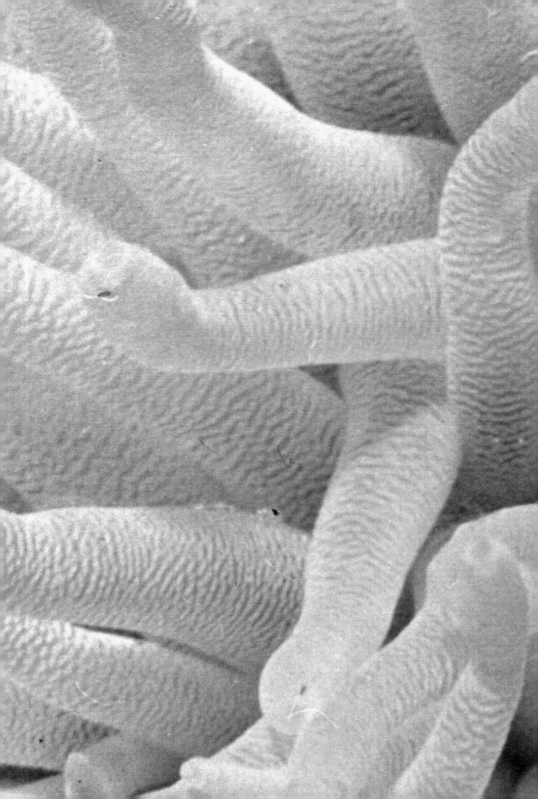

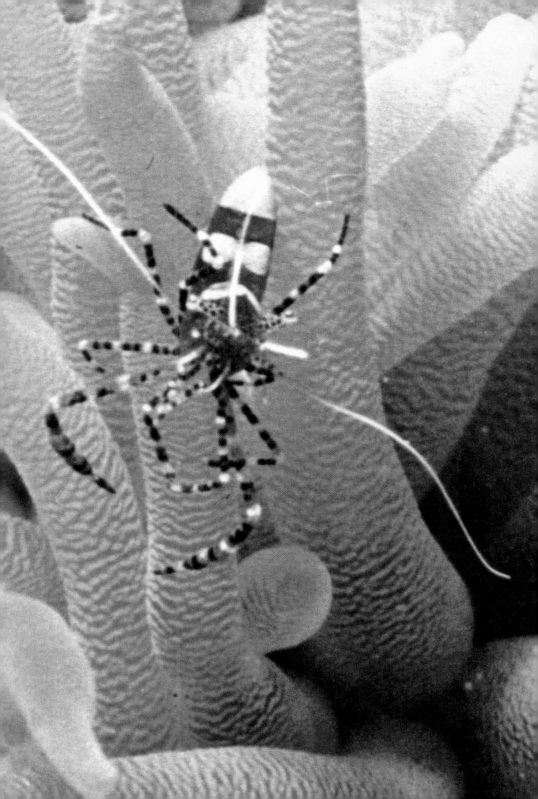

pairs of walking legs that arise below the large cephalothorax. Additional appendages are associated with the mouth as food-handling organs, and further appendages below the abdomen serve in mating or in holding the eggs until they hatch. Usually, a crustacean of this order goes through a series of larval stages among the plankton near the sea surface before transforming to the adult body form.

Free-swimming decapods are mostly known as shrimps and prawns, and ordinarily have a somewhat compressed body and rather small pincers on the anterior legs. On the commercial shrimp *(Peneus setiferus)*, found in the Gulf of Mexico, it is the third pair of legs that bears the grasping organs. On the sand shrimp *(Crangon septemspinosus)*, of intertidal and deeper Atlantic waters from North Carolina to the Arctic Ocean, it is the second pair of legs that bear claws. The West Coast shrimp *(C. franciscorum)* is similarly equipped. Although a fisherman is likely to refer to any large shrimp as a "prawn," the name is better reserved for the small members of genus *Palaemonetes*, such as *P. vulgaris*, which is abundant among eelgrass and tidal gutters from New Hampshire south along the Atlantic coast. In *Palaemonetes*, the first and second pairs of legs bear claws and the stalked compound eyes are widely separated by a strong spiny projection (rostrum) on the head, whereas in *Crangon* and *Peneus* the eyes are close together and the rostrum small.

Along the east coast of Florida south of St. Augustine and around the Gulf of Mexico, tropical shrimps *(Macrobrachium)* have established themselves in brackish and fresh waters and have even gone up the Mississippi River as far as Missouri. Often, these long-tailed crustaceans attain a length of four inches or more.

From North Carolina southward to South American coasts, the largest of the long-tailed decapods is the spiny lobster *(Panulirus argus)*, which lacks pincers altogether. Although found occasionally around the Gulf of Mexico, it is common only among the coral crevices of the Florida Keys. During the day these animals hide, but keep the extremely strong, whiplike antennae extended to detect any intruders and lash them away. At night, spiny lobsters move about in search of worms, small mollusks, and carrion. It is then that even those as long as 16 inches are caught and eaten by sharks, groupers, and jewfish.

North of North Carolina to Labrador, the lobsters are quite different— members of *Homarus*, and more like freshwater crayfishes *(Cambarus* and *Astacus)* than any other crustaceans in the sea. All of these animals have pincers

Whale Louse (Paracyamus sp.)   173
Brackish-water Shrimp (Palaemon macrodactylus)

Barbershop Shrimp (Stenopus hispidus)

Spiny Lobster (Panulirus)

on the first three pairs of walking legs. Those on the first pair are especially large and formidable as weapons of offense and defense. Muscles within the big pincers, like those within the abdomen of all long-tailed decapods, provide such delectable food that they are sought commercially in large numbers. Consequently, fewer lobsters remain to scavenge along the bottom in subtidal shallows than would live there if traps were not set out to catch them.

The long-tailed decapods which have the least muscular abdomens are the hermit crabs, which hide their vulnerable parts in the recesses of empty snail shells and carry these about with them wherever they go. Generally, a hermit crab stops to inspect, and even to test for fit, any other shell of approximately suitable size that it encounters while scavenging over the sea floor or along the beach. At the slightest disturbance, the hermit withdraws completely into its shelter. After a while, it extends its big pincers, then its slender antennae, its stalked eyes, and finally its walking legs, perhaps to right its shell if overturned, and proceeds on its way. The small hermits that live in periwinkle shells, and the larger ones in whelk shells, are generally members of genus *Pagurus*. Still bigger hermits, such as *Coenobita clypeatus*, carry around conch shells in shallow waters of coastal Florida and the West Indies.

The Short-tailed Decapods (Order Decapoda)

True crabs tend to run sidewise, "crabwise," rather than forward or backward, although they can travel rapidly in any direction. Most move swiftly enough to escape being caught or, if backed into a corner, can defend themselves. Yet both fish and shellfishermen catch these crustaceans, often leaving the hard carapace where a shell collector finds it as a trophy. Consequently, the names of crabs tend to be more widely known than those of most other crustaceans. The sponge crab *(Dromia)* is the kind most likely to be camouflaged by bits of sponge and other encrusting marine life. The calico or lady crab *(Ovalipes)*, which bears a pattern of conspicuous brown spots on its pale back, is one of the swimming crabs. These crabs include also the blue crab *(Callinectes sapidus)*, which is harvested commercially along the Atlantic coast from Cape Cod southward, and the green crab *(Carcinides maenas)* that is found both in marine and brackish environments, often preying upon small bivalves. A blue crab that has recently molted its shell in a pen is sold as a "soft-shell" crab, as though it were a different kind.

The "rock" crab *(Cancer)* has been made famous by the stellar constellation named for it, and the zodiacal sign shown in the almanac; it is as often found

176   *Large Hermit Crab (Coenobita clypeatus)*
Green Crab (Carcinides maenas) eating a Polychaete Worm (Glycera sp.)

on sandy and muddy subtidal bottoms as among rocks along the coast. Mud crabs, such as *Panopeus*, move about more slowly than most short-tailed decapods and live primarily on mud flats. Pea crabs, such as *Pinnotheres*, are often found in the mantle cavities of freshly opened bivalves in which they take shelter or live for extended times, apparently feeding on the larger particles of organic matter brought in by the water current created by the mollusk. Spider crabs, which have stouter, longer legs and smaller pincers than most crabs, stay where the coastal waters have full salinity. *Libinia* is often common along muddy and sandy shores, whereas the Alaska king crab *(Paralithodes camtschatica)* prefers depths exceeding 40 feet around the northernmost coasts of the North Pacific Ocean.

A number of different crabs have become almost terrestrial as adults. The ghost crab *(Ocypoda quadrata)* digs U- or Y-shaped burrows in the beach from Long Island Sound to Rio de Janeiro, emerging at night to scavenge along the shores. Often the characteristic tracks of this pale-bodied, fast-moving crab are found converging to a burrow opening. By day the crab may plug its doorway with sand. At the northern end of its range, the ghost crabs hibernate deep in burrows far up the beach, in dunes where only waves from violent waves will come.

From Georgia southward and around the Gulf of Mexico, land crabs *(Gecarcinus lateralis)* pock the shores with their burrows, particularly among mangrove roots and other vegetation that reinforces the soil. Fiddler crabs *(Uca)* make smaller holes, and range up the Atlantic coast as far as Cape Cod, as well as along sandy and muddy shores of southern California and into brackish tidal gutters that penetrate saltmarshes. Fiddler crabs are active primarily by day when the tide is out, and often feed from exposed sand flats in great armies. Among them, the males can be recognized from a distance, each bearing one huge pincer (the "fiddle") used in defense and in courtship gestures, and one small pincer with which to pick up food. Females have two small pincers, and feed ambidextrously. Males are right- or left-handed, but change if they lose a big pincer. At the next molt, they regenerate a big pincer where the small one was before, and a small one where the big one was lost. Consequently about 50 per cent of the males are right-handed.

The Mantis Shrimps (Order Stomatopoda)

Lurking in small holes in the sea floor, particularly where the water is less than 100 feet deep, about 200 different kinds of mantis shrimps comprising the little order Stomatopoda have evolved into some of the world's most alert marine predators. At first glance a mantis shrimp appears to be a type of lobster, because it has the same sturdy cylindrical body, muscular abdomen ending in a fanshaped tail that can be cupped quickly for backward locomotion, and several pairs of thoracic appendages which serve as walking legs. But the mantis shrimp has only a short carapace and its second pair of legs are highly specialized "jackknife claws." With them, a stomatopod can snatch a passing fish and cut it into pieces, which it then eats in the seclusion of its burrow.

The large mantis shrimp *(Squilla empusa)* of the Atlantic coast is 12 inches long. With its prehensile claws it can inflict serious wounds on anyone handling it carelessly, and also jab effectively with the sharp spines that project beyond the edge of its sturdy tail fin. The smaller *Pseudosquilla* of the Pacific coast, and the 3-inch *Gonodactylus oerstedii* found along Atlantic shores from North Carolina to Brazil are more common.

The Centipedes (Class Chilopoda)

Most "hundred-legged worms" that one comes upon have only 15 pairs of legs. Each pair of legs arises from a separate segment of the elongated body, at the front of which is a distinct head with a single pair of antennae.

Alaska King Crab (Paralithodes camtschatica)

Atlantic Ghost Crab (Ocypode quadrata)

Almost all of the 2,800 different kinds of centipedes are terrestrial predators, but only members of the order Scutigeromorpha, to which the house centipede *(Cermatia forceps)* belongs, have compound eyes. This creature has an almost globular head and long legs; it feeds on household insects. Stone centipedes, such as the reddish brown *Lithobius forficatus* that sometimes gets into damp basements, have short legs with the last two pairs trailing behind. Glands on the final pair secrete sticky droplets that repel pursuing beetles.

All centipedes are armed with a pair of poison claws alongside the mouth. These make the larger members of the order Scolopendromorpha dangerous when handled. *Scolopendra viridus*, which is khaki-colored and has 21 to 23 pairs of black-tipped yellow legs, grows to a length of 5 inches and is found in the southeastern United States. In Arizona, *S. heros* attains 6 inches and is strikingly colored blue-black at each end of the earth-brown body, and has orange

Overleaf: top, Stone Centipede (Lithobius sp.); bottom, Blind Centipede with eggs (Geophilus sp.); right, Eastern Woodland Millipedes (Pseudopolydesmus sp.)

Arizona Centipede (Scolopendra heros)

antennae. Although these centipedes move slowly, they sometimes attack and kill frogs and toads, then feed on the victim when it dies of the venom.

Soil centipedes, which move even more deliberately, are the only members of this class that may have 100 legs. Like other centipedes, they hatch from the egg with no more than 15 pairs of legs but gradually add extra leg-bearing segments until the total may be anywhere from 31 to 181 pairs. The common blind species of *Geophilus* and *Arenophilus* grow to a length of almost two inches and have 91 pairs of legs; they explore earthworm tunnels and other passageways through the soil as far as 30 inches underground in search of mites, springtails, insect larvae, and small worms.

The Millipedes (Class Diplopoda)

Waves of activity proceed from the posterior end of a millipede as it glides along, lifting its many pairs of legs in turn and moving them forward to set them down and swing them back before repeating the cycle. But even the longest and slimmest of millipedes have no more than 250 pairs of legs, and most of the common kinds possess fewer than 50 pairs. Usually, the first segment behind the head has none, the next three segments have one pair each, and the following segments (actually double segments) have two pairs apiece.

Most millipedes are harmless scavengers, feeding on decaying plant material. Relatively few of the 7,200 species are found outside the tropical rain forests, but these few include representatives of several orders and some kinds that can defend themselves by secreting hydrocyanic acid. The eyeless polydesmids (order Polydesmida) bear a prominent lateral ridge on each segment that makes the body appear flat or only mildly convex above; a 1-inch species *(Oxidus gracilus)* has become cosmopolitan as the "greenhouse millipede," although it is native to the tropics; in California, *Luminodesmus sequoiae* is luminous, for no known reason. Compound eyes and a cylindrical body are usual among members of the order Juliformia, which includes the introduced Eurasian *Diploiulus londinensis*, a burrower that becomes a garden pest in wet weather by attacking the young seedlings and subterranean roots and tubers of plants. Called a "wireworm," it will often curl its 1-inch body like a watchspring if disturbed, as will also the native 4-inch *Narceus (Spirobolus) americanus* found in rotting logs from Texas to eastern Canada.

The Symphylans (Class Symphyla)

Among the kin of millipedes are members of a small class with only 120 species, one of which *(Scutigerella immaculata)* sometimes becomes a pest in greenhouses and gardens. Known as the garden centipede, it is only about 1/3 inch long, with pale, threadlike antennae, 12 pairs of walking legs, and a terminal pair of spinnerets. Unlike any other centipede or millipede, the little animal moves all legs on one side simultaneously in a curious waddling gait. Unfortunately, it often forsakes its diet of dead plant material to attack living plants that man cherishes. Of all the many-legged arthropods, the symphylans may be most nearly like the ancestral form from which insects evolved.

The Horseshoe "Crabs" (Class Merostomata)

Along the Atlantic coast from the Bay of Fundy to Key West, and at scattered places around the Gulf of Mexico to Yucatan, lives the horseshoe "crab," *Limulus polyphemus*, an animal whose ancestry shows little change for at least

175 million years. Today its only surviving relatives are three species in Oriental waters. All of them are strongly armored, with a huge convex cephalothorax shaped like a horse's hoof. Behind this is hinged a trapezoidal one-piece abdomen followed by a movable tail spine. The carapace may be 26 inches across and the overall length to the tip of the tail approach 40 inches.

Unlike crustaceans, centipedes, millipedes, and insects, which have antennae and paired jaws, a horseshoe "crab" lacks both antennae and jaws, thereby revealing its kinship to scorpions and spiders of class Arachnida. Below the cephalothorax, the most anterior pair of appendages are pincer-like chelicerae with only three segments. They serve to guide food to the mouth, which is deep among the spiny bases of the five pairs of legs. With these spines the animal shreds the seaweed and marine animals on which it feeds. The first four pairs of legs have pincers, while the fifth pair bears projections, like the ring on a ski pole, preventing the sharp point from going too far into the substratum. Below the abdomen are hinged flaps protecting and concealing the leaflike gills. The horseshoe crab uses these flaps as well as its legs when swimming, which it does in an inverted position. After a bout of swimming, the animal usually settles to the bottom back downward and then uses its tail spine to right itself.

In the spring of the year, horseshoe "crabs" move from deeper water to coastal shallows and there pair up. The males are usually smaller than their mates and use a modified claw on each of the first pair of walking legs to cling to the posterior corners of the female's abdominal shell. She tows him around wherever she goes until after she has bulldozed a "nest" in the sand near the high-tide mark and deposited her eggs in it. Before letting go, he floods the water with fertilizing milt. After a few weeks, the tailless young seem to explode from their egg membranes and work their way to the sand surface while high tide is washing over them. Thereafter they grow, molt by molt, becoming larger and more heavily armored and like their parents in body form. Unlike any other arthropods, horseshoe "crabs" molt by splitting their external skeleton around the front rim of the cephalothorax and creeping out of the slit. Cast shells that appear intact, although utterly empty, are often cast ashore, where beachcombers find them.

The Spiders and Their Kin (Class Arachnida)

The familiar spiders and the less widely known scorpions, whip scorpions or whipspiders, sun spiders, pseudoscorpions, harvestmen, mites, and ticks com-

Ornate Western Millipede (Sigmoria sp.)
Spirostreptid Millipede (Orthoporus sp.)

prise an enormously interesting, although generally abhorred, group of animals whose ancestry can be traced back to the Silurian period more than 400 million years ago. Lacking antennae and jaws, they subsist on liquid nourishment, mostly squeezed and sucked from insect prey. The body bears a pair of chelicerae beside the mouth, a pair of modified legs, called pedipalpi, used in sensing and handling food, and four pairs of walking legs. The abdomen may be conspicuously segmented and flexible, as in scorpions, or unsegmented and set off from the cephalothorax by a narrow waist, as in spiders, or joined broadly as an indistinct part of a compact body, as in harvestmen, mites, and ticks. Generally the abdomen bears one or two ventral openings, admitting air to leaflike respiratory organs called book lungs. The abdomen also has, posteriorly a group of specialized appendages known as spinnerets, with which silk fibers secreted by several glands are formed into webs of various kinds. The name of the class comes from Arachne, a Lydian girl who supposedly challenged the Greek goddess Athena to a contest in weaving ability and was changed into a spider for her arrogance.

The Scorpions (Order Scorpionida)

The most evident features of the 700 different kinds of scorpions are the pincer-style pedipalpi and the venomous stinger at the tip of the abdomen. Less than 30 species of these animals inhabit North America, most of them in the warm, arid Southwest. The largest of them in the country are members of genus *Centruroides*, of which the rather plain brown *C. sculpturatus* of Arizona—almost 3 inches long—is justly feared for its poison. A darker brown species *(C. gracilis)*, with pale walking legs, reaches similar dimensions and is found from Texas to Florida, but like the somewhat smaller and more black-and-yellow *C. hentzi* and *C. vittatus* of Florida and the adjacent states, it secretes a less potent venom. The large hairy *Hadrurus hirsutus*, which grows to be 4 inches long, found in the southwestern states, varies considerably in color, often being pastel green with bluish legs and tail. The same colors may mark the striped-tailed *Vejovis spinigerus* (2 to 3 inches long) in the Southwest, and a yellower hue the 2-inch *V. boreus* of the western States and southern Alberta—the only scorpion to reach Canada. All of these animals are active in the dark and hide by day. They merely grasp small prey in their pedipalpi while kneading it with the chelicerae and sucking its juices. Scorpions subdue larger victims by prodding them with the stinger, while the slender, flexible abdomen is curled up and forward over the scorpion's back.

Horseshoe Crab (Limulus polyphemus) with Acron Barnacles (Balanus sp.)

Overleaf: top left, Florida Scorpion (Centruroides sp.); bottom left, Western Scorpion (Uroctonus mordax); right, Vinegarone (Mastigoproctus giganteus)

The Whip Scorpions (Order Uropygi)

These members of order Uropygi appear formidable enough, and can pinch in self defense with their large pedipalpi. The first pair of walking legs are somewhat elongated, slender, and flexible; they are used like antennae to explore ahead of the animal and to examine potential prey by touch and odor. The vinegarone *(Mastigoproctus giganteus)*, of the southern United States from Florida to Arizona, grows to be more than 3 inches long, and bears a slender jointed tail that is often turned up over the back like that of a scorpion, although it has no stinger. Instead, these nocturnal animals can spray a vinegar-scented mist from a gland at the base of the tail, apparently as a means of softening the skeletons of insects that are to be squeezed of their juices and as a repellent for predatory birds such as desert owls. Florida has also a 1/2-inch representative of the tropical tailless whip scorpions (order Amblypygi), which have much longer whiplike front legs but no tail. Correctly known as *Tarantula marginemaculata* and placed in the family Tarantulidae, this animal is no relation to the European wolf spider *(Lycosa tarantula)* whose bite was supposedly counteracted by dancing the tarentelle, or to the tropical hairy theraphosid spider that occasionally reaches temperate cities in bunches of bananas and is feared as though its bite were in proportion to its 2- to 3-inch body.

The True Spiders (Order Araneae or Araneida)

The theraphosid spiders may actually earn their name of "bird spiders" by occasionally capturing a small bird. About 30 different kinds live in the United States, mostly in the Southwest. Some of the species of *Aphonopelma* grow to a body length of nearly 3 inches and a leg span of about 6 inches. Their nearest kin are the trapdoor spiders (family Ctenizidae), which are rarely longer than 1 inch. Ctenizids use a spiny rake on their chelicerae to dig a tubular cavity in the soil or the bark of a tree, and line it with silk. The Californian *Bothriocyrtum* dig vertical burrows and cap them with a hinged cover. *Ummidia* species in the southeastern states dig almost horizontal tubes into river banks. *Antrodiaetus* makes a vertical tube with a projecting flexible rim that can be pursed together for privacy; these spiders can be found from Alaska to the Gulf of Mexico, but rarely grow more than 1/2 inch in body length.

The spiders most properly feared in North America are the brown recluse spider *(Loxosceles reclusa)* of the family Loxoscelidae, which has been expanding its range recently from Texas northward and eastward, and the black widow

Theraphosid "Tarantula" (Aphonopelma eutylenum) with cricket prey

(Latrodectus mactans), a cobweb weaver of family Theridiidae. Females of both species associate extremely intimately with people, building loose webs in houses and outbuildings, staying close to the eggs they hang in sacs within the web. If disturbed, the spiders bite. In both the venom is particularly poisonous, and the fangs on the chelicerae deliver the dose under the skin where its effect is rapid and often dangerous—particularly to a child or an infirm adult. The 1-inch brown recluse is a 6-eyed spider with a undistinguished shape and coloration. The 2/3-inch black widow female is almost solid black, with a spherical abdomen below which has a bright red marking usually shaped like an hourglass. This species, which has eight eyes like most spiders, is found from Oregon to New Hampshire and southward into tropical America. It belongs to one of the largest families of spiders, with more than 200 species in North America. They include less dangerous members of *Latrodectes*, which remain outdoors, and the harmless, common, American house spider *(Achae-*

Overleaf: left, Orb-web Spider, underside (Araneus sp.); top right, Silver Orb-web Spider (Argiope argentata); bottom right, Long-jawed Orb-web Spider (Tetragnatha sp.)

Black Widow Spider (Latrodectus mactans)

aranea tepidariorum, which has become cosmopolitan—to the dismay of house-wives who find its dust-laden webs and brown egg packets hung in window corners and many other quiet parts of the home. The spider measures about 1/3 inch if a female and 1/5 inch if a male; the abdomen has the same globular form as that of the black widow, but is tan marked with patches and streaks of dark gray.

The European house spiders *(Tegenaria)* have become almost cosmopolitan. They are twice as large as the American kinds and belong to the family Age-lenidae, more commonly called the funnel weavers, whose native species in the United States and Canada are commonly known as grass spiders. They produce nearly horizontal sheets of web upon the short-cut grass, leading to a shelter tunnel to one side. From the tunnel the spider dashes out at any insect that crosses the web. The web itself becomes most noticeable in late summer when coated by morning dew. Cobwebs in the cellar, however, are likely to be the work of still different spiders, such as the 1/3-inch long-bodied cellar spider *(Pholcus phalangioides)*, whose legs earn it the name daddy-long-legs; it is a member of the Pholcidae, and no relation to a harvestman. Often a female is seen carrying her spherical mass of eggs in her chelicerae. In the southern United States, a much larger house spider is the 1-inch huntsman *(Heteropoda venatoria)*, which commonly emerges from a daytime hideaway at dusk to stand in plain sight on a wall, waiting for a cockroach or other household insect to come near. Seldom does the huntsman make a web of any kind. Females carry their egg sacs below the mouth until the young hatch out.

The orb-web weavers of family Argiopidae are more universally admired, at least outside the house. The 3/4-inch garden spider *(Araneus diadematus)* has a pattern of white spots in the shape of a cross on its abdomen. It waits at the edge of its web until some insect blunders into the sticky spiral lines. The black-and-yellow *Argiope aurantia* grows a 1-inch body and clings head down to the center of the orb web, which usually has a zigzag band of white silk as reinforcement. In Florida and warmer parts of the New World, the 1-inch golden silk spider *(Nephila clavipes)* constructs orb webs 5 to 10 feet across between trees, with support strands strong enough to hold a big moth or a hummingbird.

Cellar Spider (Pholcus phalangioides) with egg mass

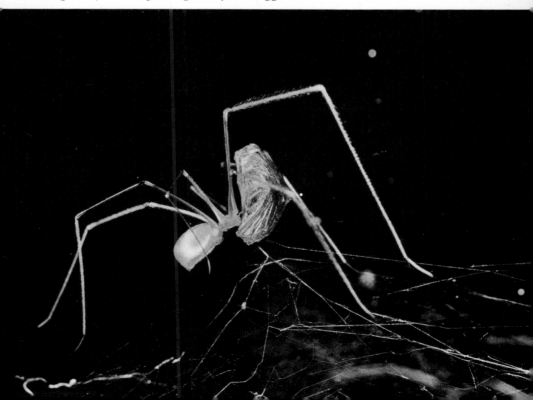

Webs are of far less importance to the hunting spiders of family Lycosidae, which carry their spherical egg sacs attached to the spinnerets until their young emerge and are carried on their mother's back. This is the habit of the wolf spiders *(Lycosa)* that often hunt over the forest floor at night, and of the pale-bodied *Arctosa* spiders that are so perfectly camouflaged on sea-beach sand, and the members of the genus *Pardosa* that are the most common arachnids at high altitudes and high latitudes. The related fishing spiders *(Dolomedes)* of family Pisauridae carry their egg masses in their chelicerae, under the body, even when they run across the water surface of a pond or slow stream; when the young are about to hatch, however, the mother makes a nursery web by tying leaves together and waits beside them until the young go off on their own. Crab spiders, such as *Misumena vatia,* which is often seen crouching in a flower while waiting for a fly or bee to pause within reach, generally die before their young emerge, but the males sometimes show a different use for silk by wrapping a prospective mate loosely as part of his courtship antics.

The special acrobats are the jumping spiders of family Salticidae, of which North America has about 300 species. They are active by day, leaping from one perch to another or jumping atop an insect from a distance of many times their own length. The common black-and-silver *Salticus scenicus* is often seen about buildings, and noticed despite its 1/5-inch length. Larger species in the southern United States are easier to follow and especially entertaining when performing elaborate courtship dances which their fine eyes make meaningful.

The Sun Spiders (Order Solpulgida or Solifugae)

In arid areas of the Great Plains and the southern States, yellowish or brown arachnids of order *Solpulgida* live in shallow burrows. From these they run out and back in so swiftly that it is often hard to see the pointed, forceps-like chelicerae reaching straight ahead, the leglike pedipalpi and first pair of legs raised and used as sense organs, and the six legs on which the sun spider darts out to seize prey. One 4/5-inch species *(Ammotrechella stimpsoni)* lives in Florida and the West Indies. Another 120 kinds are native to western North America, and include some an inch long. They bite but lack venom.

The Pseudoscorpions (Order Pseudoscorpionida)

Only one among almost 200 species of these members of order Pseudoscorpionida is likely to be noticed by most people: the house pseudoscorpion *(Chelifer cancroides).* With a body only 1/5-inch long and no tail or stinger, it reaches

Preceding page: left, Southwestern Jumping Spider (Phidippus sp.); top right, Funnel-web Grass Spider (Angelenopsis sp.); center right, Wolf Spider with young (Lycosa sp.); bottom right, Orb Weaver (Neoscona arabesca)

Daddy-long-legs or Harvestman Spider (Family Phalangiidae)

out long, strong pedipalpi that end in pincers and contain minute poison glands. Yet so flat is the creature that it can slip easily into cracks, often in pursuit of mites and small insects the householder would gladly do without. This is a cosmopolitan species. Other pseudoscorpions tend to be widespread too.

The Harvestmen (Order Opiliones or Phalangida)

North America has about 200 different members of the order Opiliones, mostly in the family Phalangiidae, which typically have extremely slender long legs on a compact, broad-waisted body. The body itself is only about 1/2-inch long on the largest of these arachnids, but the legs may spread out over an area more than 3 inches in diameter. Harvestmen feed on small insects, or sometimes on carrion and plant juices. Country people have long claimed that if a harvestman is held gently with its front legs free, it will point to where the cows are.

The Mites and Ticks (Order Acarina or Acari)

The most varied of arachnids are the members of order Acarina. In these the segmental pattern of body structure is almost obliterated, so that the location

Velvet Mite (Trombidium sp.)

of the legs, pedipalps, chelicerae and eyes (if any) are the principal features and even a head is so ill-marked that the region around the mouth is called merely the "capitulum." Except for one group, all of which are external parasites on reptiles, birds or mammals and known as ticks (suborder Ixodides), the members of this order are called mites; most of them are less than 1/50 inch in length. As adults they have four pairs of legs, but their larvae begin with only three pairs.

Some mites are free-living predators in the soil, or on the surfaces of plants, eating tinier insects or insect eggs. Others, such as the harvestmites of family Trombiculidae are parasites as larvae, and predators as adults; almost 50 species in this family attack human skin and are known as chiggers, causing severe itching and carrying diseases such as scrub typhus fever. Water mites are often larger, up to 1/10 inch and velvety red as they swim about in ponds; some parasitize bivalves or aquatic insects. Still other mites live only as parasites, such as the chicken mite *(Dermanyssus gallinae)* which attacks poultry and poultrymen. Some terrestrial mites cause plants to produce blister-like galls inside of which the mites hide and feed. Horticulturalists find many kinds of *Tetranychus* to be "red spider mites" attacking foliage and fruits, causing economic losses. The cheese mite *(Acarus siro)* feeds on stored cheeses and causes an allergic reaction known as "grocer's itch." Domestic animals and man may suffer from attacks of the mange mite *(Sarcoptes scabei).*

Most ticks enlarge spectacularly as they gorge themselves with blood, and drop off their host after feeding. The legs, which total 3 pairs in immature ticks and 4 pairs in adults, are used only for locomotion and for holding to vegetation where a suitable host may pass. The hooklike teeth in the mouth become the sole organs of attachment. In the soft ticks, such as *Ornithodoros hermsi* (which parasitizes wild rodents but transmits the spirochaete of relapsing fever to man), the body is leathery with no hard plates, and the mouth is underneath. In the hard ticks, a hard plate covers the head region and the mouthparts are directed forward. The widespread rabbit tick *(Haemaphysalis leporispalustris)* of North America, which is less than 1/10 inch long until gorged, is important in transmitting the bacteria of tularemia. The western wood tick *(Dermacentor ander-*

Sea Spider (Class Pycnogonida)

soni) became famous in the Rocky Mountain region as the carrier of the rickettsia causing spotted fever; until it has had a blood meal from some large mammal or a person, it is about 1/5 inch long and seems extremely flat. The brown tick *(Rhipicephalus sanguineus)* which is found in houses man shares with a dog, is about the same size and almost cosmopolitan; it rarely bites man, but feeds regularly on the dog. In cattle country of the American Southwest, the largest tick is ordinarily the cattle tick *(Boophilus annulatus)*, of which engorged females may be more than an inch long; it transmits the sporozoan parasite causing Texas cattle fever.

The Sea Spiders *(Class Pycnogonida)*

Among the most peculiar of marine animals are the slow-moving, clinging predators called sea spiders. Each has a small, three-part trunk with an anterior proboscis, usually a pair each of chelicerae and palps close to the proboscis, and paired lateral projections bearing from 4 to 6 pairs of long, jointed walking legs that may end in sharp claws. Close to the base of the first pair of legs, the male (at least) has an additional pair of ventral appendages known as ovigerous legs; they are used by him to carry the two egg masses produced by his mate, or even more masses if he has mated several times in succession with additional females. Sea spiders feed on hydroids, anemones, moss animals and sponges.

Only the order Pantopoda is represented by the more than 500 species of sea spiders known today. Of these, at least a dozen kinds are found in coastal waters of North America. A broad flat body, no chelicerae or palps or claws, are features of the 2/3-inch *Pycnogonum littorale* that creeps about on encrusted stones near the low-tide mark from Long Island Sound northward along the Atlantic coast, and the rather similar *P. stearnsi* found in similar locations from California north on the Pacific side. Species of *Achelia* have an almost disc-shaped body, with both chelicerae and palps beside the proboscis and claws tipping each walking leg.

The Arrow Worms *(Phylum Chaetognatha)*

Like animated toothpicks, the arrow worms dart about in sea water. They prey upon minute crustaceans, the larvae of many other animals, including fish, and

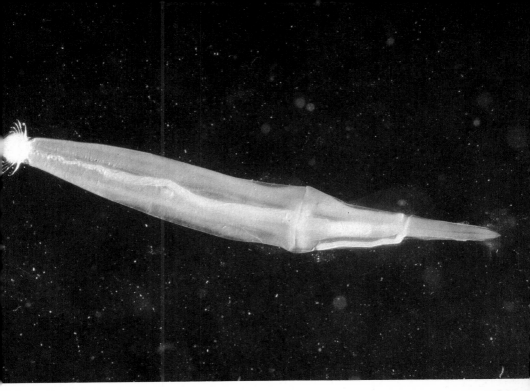

Arrow Worm (Sagitta sp.)

take also quite an assortment of protozoans and algal cells. Each arrow worm is cylindrical, from 3/4 to 4 inches long, and barely 1/8 inch in diameter even across its narrow lateral fins. A tail fin of comparable breadth and in the same plane may draw attention to the post-anal tail, which is a familiar feature of chordates but is possessed by no other invertebrate animals. On each side of the slit-shaped mouth, an arrow worm has a muscular lobe bearing conspicuous grasping spines and some rows of small teeth. The phylum name (the "bristle mouths") refers to these jawlike lobes with their spines.

The arrow worm twitches its longitudinal muscles to propel itself forward or backward through the water. Often this movement is too fast for the human eye to follow. The glassy transparency of the body generally makes detailed observations difficult, but the location of the arrow worm may be revealed because undigested food in its straight digestive tract is still opaque. Actually, the body cavity is capacious, lined by a ciliated peritoneum and hence a coelom, and divided by partitions into compartments: a pair in the head, a pair in the trunk, and one or two in the tail. The trunk contains both ovaries and testes, for all arrow worms are hermaphrodites. Apparently the free-living, pelagic species engage in self-fertilization and either release their developing eggs to drift in the sea or attach them to their own bodies and carry them a while.

One genus *(Spadella)* consists of sedentary species with stocky bodies and adhesive structures on fingerlike projections situated either just in front of the tail fin or on the fin itself. These animals show cross-fertilization, and cement their eggs to the sea floor or the bottom of a tide pool. Often a *Spadella* waits until prey is within snatching distance, and feeds without letting go of its support.

The planktonic arrow worms avoid contact with solid objects but are often abundant close to shore. *Sagitta*, the largest genus, has species with two pairs of lateral fins. *Eukrohnia* has a long slender neck region, and *Pterosagitta* a thick-necked appearance because of a massive collar-like fold around the head; members of both genera have a single pair of small lateral fins. Differences in the teeth and grasping spines are used to tell one kind of arrow worm from another.

The Echinoderms *(Phylum Echinodermata)*

To most people it seems logical that the distinguished 19th-century zoologist Baron Georges Cuvier classified the sea stars ("starfishes"), sea urchins and other echinoderms along with the medusae ("jellyfishes") and sea anemones as Radiate Animals ("phylum Radiata"). These creatures differ from most other animals in having a radial rather than a bilateral symmetry. Yet today, the echinoderms are accorded a phylum of their own and widely separated from the medusae and sea anemones of phylum Cnidaria (or Coelenterata). Features of embryonic development, of the tissue (peritoneum) that lines the body cavity, and of intimate chemistry are believed to indicate that echinoderms are related more closely to chordates than to any other phylum.

Unlike chordates, all echinoderms are marine. Most are associated with the sea floor, or with rocky, sandy and muddy bottoms along the coasts. Habitually, these animals move slowly from place to place or remain at one site. Very few are able to swim, and none run or fly. Apparently this has been their way of life for more than 600 million years, for closely similar animals left fossil remains in sediments of the early Cambrian period. Fossilization was made probable by a limy skeleton beneath the skin, often showing plates and pores in patterns that are totally unlike any produced by a vertebrate.

Members of five different classes may be found living along North American coasts: the sea lilies and feather stars; the sea cucumbers; the sea urchins and sand dollars; the sea stars; and the serpent stars. They show varying degrees of development of a unique echinoderm feature: a water-vascular system with soft, fluid-filled, muscular tube-feet.

The Sea Lilies and Feather Stars (Class Crinoidea)

Until animals in 10 to 60 feet of water lost their privacy because divers equipped with face mask and snorkel or SCUBA equipment began to visit them, the members of this class were generally regarded as living beyond the reach of human fingers. Most sea lilies do remain in the deep sea, beyond the continental shelves, each individual with its supporting stalk atop which is a flower-like body. The imitation petals are actually five branching arms, spread to catch small particles of organic matter sinking through the water. Small tube-feet push the particles into a rope of mucus secreted and moved along grooves in the arms to the central mouth, which faces upward.

Feather stars in shallower water start life in this same attached way and then, as they mature, free themselves forever from the stalk. They either cling to some rocky support by means of a ring of movable spines where the stalk broke off, or swim by ponderous up-and-down movements of the outstretched branching arms. Several tropical species with these habits are found on coral reefs of the Florida Keys and at various places around the Gulf of Mexico. A cold-tolerant feather star *(Antedon)*, which seems extremely delicate because it sheds pieces of its arms when handled, lives at a depth of 30 feet or more in Long Island Sound but in progressively shallower water northward to the Arctic, and down European coasts. North Pacific species seem not to come near the surface, but show the same capacity to escape by self-mutilation followed by rapid regeneration of missing parts.

The Sea Cucumbers (Class Holothuria)

Unlike other echinoderms, sea cucumbers are elongate animals with the mouth at one end connected by a long tubular intestine to the anus at the other end. The body wall is flexible, reinforced by no more than microscopic plates, but kept turgid by the pressure of fluid within the body cavity. Usually the animal lies on one side, extending retractable tentacles from around the mouth into

Sea Cucumber (Parastichopus californicus)
208

surface sediments to pick up organic particles which are then sucked off when each tentacle in turn is thrust into the mouth. Most sea cucumbers make more conspicuous movements at the posterior end, where they inhale and exhale sea water through the muscular cloaca, from which branching tubes known as respiratory trees extend far into the body cavity.

Creeping slowly about on the bottom of muddy shallows, members of *Thyone* in brown or olive-green or black sometimes attain a length of 5 inches. Over the body, a soft pilelike covering of short projections obscures the radial pattern of inner structures, for the projections are tube-feet arising almost randomly. In *Cucumaria*, which often grows to be 12 inches long and 3 to 4 inches in diameter, the lower surface bears three lengthwise double rows of well-developed tube-feet but the two corresponding double rows on the upper surface are reduced and almost functionless. *Cucumaria* lives in cooler water along the Atlantic and Pacific coasts, whereas *Thyone* is found in the Gulf of Mexico too. The related species of *Psolus* around all coasts of North America have lost the tube-feet from all body areas except a creeping sole on the underside.

The 10 bushy tentacles of a *Thyone* or a *Cucumaria* can be withdrawn completely into the body, whereas those of the giant tropical and subtropical sea cucumbers *Holothuria* and *Stichopus* are about twice as numerous and expanded at the tips, which prevents them from being retracted. Instead, the big sea cucumbers (which may be 18 inches long and 8 inches in diameter) use their soft tentacles to push mud into their mouths. Consequently, they pass through their digestive tracts enormous quantities of undigestible material. To measure these quantities, the late Professor W. J. Crozier of Harvard University set collecting dishes under the cloacal ends of several *Stichopus badionotus* on coral sand in shallow water on a Bermuda coast and weighed the sand particles that rained down from the animals in an hour. Multiplying this total by the number of sea cucumbers on an acre of sandy bottom and by the number of hours in a year, he concluded that each one filtered the organic matter out of 200 to 300 pounds of surface sediments annually.

Stichopus and *Holothuria* seem particularly sensitive to being molested at their cloacal ends by, for example, foraging crabs. The sea cucumbers react vigorously by turning their cloacal regions and often their respiratory trees inside out and discharging long sticky threads of secretion from glands in the walls of these organs. The threads entangle and immobilize a crab or a fish. The echinoderm makes no attempt to withdraw its parts afterward, but sheds them by self-mutilation, even though this means severing the posterior part of the

Overleaf: left, Feather Star (Family Antedonidae); top right, Red Sea Cucumber (Cucumaria miniata); bottom right, Purple (Strongylocentrotus purpuratus) and Red (S. franciscanus) Sea Urchins

intestine and opening the body cavity broadly to the ocean. Evisceration is followed quickly by regeneration. In waters of Puget Sound, at least, the common *Parastichopus californicus* seems to carry this amazing process one step farther by eviscerating spontaneously once a year and then rebuilding its cloaca, respiratory organs and part of its intestine.

The most efficient sediment-movers among sea cucumbers are the tailed kinds known as molpadonias, which remain completely buried in sandy mud below the low-tide mark, with only the cloacal opening (with five small clusters of tubefeet) and a flexible tail projecting. A single individual, with a body no more than 7 inches long and a 3-inch tail, may move 125 to 150 pounds of sedimentary material through its digestive tract in the course of a year.

The Sea Urchins and Sand Dollars (Class Echinoidea)

Of all the skeletons produced by echinoderms, those of the sea urchins, heart urchins and sand dollars attract by far the most attention when they are cast up upon the beach and dried in the sun. The thin dark skin of the urchins peels off, revealing fitted limy plates in a handsome pattern, many of them perforated where, in the living animal, tube-feet and other organs were located. The shell of a sea urchin resembles a doorknob studded with low rounded knobs in rows where stiff spines were attached, each with its own ball-and-socket joint. Otherwise the shell is almost uniformly thin, with a single circular opening below, through which the living urchin extends the five sharp teeth of its strange mouth apparatus. The shell of a heart urchin or of a sand dollar, by contrast, is reinforced internally by a large number of struts and its upper surface bears a distinctive pattern resembling a 5-petalled flower.

In the warm waters around southern Florida and southward, tropical sea urchins are commonest where they find some protection in broadly open cavities of coral reefs. There the black hatpin urchin *(Diadema antillarum)* attains a diameter of almost 6 inches, with many slender spines fully 10 inches long. Although lacking eyes of any kind, the hatpin urchin is extremely sensitive to any change in the intensity of light reaching its globular body, and quickly turns many of its sharp brittle spines in the direction of a fish or other moving object that casts the slightest shadow on it. Shorter spines around the mouth below the body support the urchin on the sand, and allow it to move about on the yielding surface.

Small sea urchins in these same warm waters and as far north as the coast

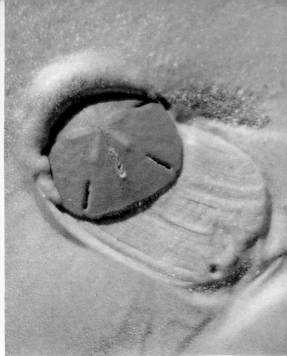

West Coast (Dendraster excentricus) and Keyhole (Melitta quinquiesperforata) Sand Dollars

of North Carolina wear spines of two sizes over the exposed parts of the body. The longer and thicker spines of these cidarid urchins have blunt tips and are clothed with a hairy coat, to which bryozoans (moss animals), small hydroids and tiny algae often become attached. The shorter, more slender and pointed spines of a cidarid are glossy and unfouled. They serve as a second line of defense against any predator that nuzzles through the camouflage of growth borne by the thick blunt spines. *Eucidaris tribuloides,* which has a diameter of 2-1/4 inches. is an attractive urchin when all of its coating is cleaned away and the encircling bands of tan and ivory color on its thick spines can be admired.

People who have emigrated from Mediterranean countries to North America are more likely to seek out the short-spined, large-bodied urchins of genus *Strongylocentrotus,* which are often abundant in cool coastal waters from Cape Cod, Massachusetts, northward and along similar shores of the North Pacific Ocean. Particularly in the spring of the year, an urchin of this type contains a generous amount of nourishment in the form of minute eggs that fill its multiple ovaries or sperm within an equal number of swollen testes. Known as "sea eggs," these urchins can be broken open and their contents cooked, or

Overleaf: left, Blood Star Fish (Henricia sanguinolenta); top right, Pacific Star Fish; bottom right, Sun Stars (Solaster endeca)

their reproductive organs can be eaten raw. The northern Atlantic, Arctic, and North Pacific species is a green urchin as much as 3-1/2 inches in diameter, and bears the scientific name of *S. dröbachiensis*, whereas a Pacific kind, *S. franciscanus*, grows almost seven inches across and varies greatly in color. Both feed primarily on brown seaweeds, to which they cling with their many slender tube-feet while rasping out small particles with their sharp teeth.

South of Cape Cod, the commonest sea urchin is the purple *Arbacia punctulata*, the shell of which is almost hidden under the covering of long, short, and medium-sized spines. Because mature, 2-inch specimens (with many 1-inch spines) were readily available to embryologists studying at the Marine Biological Laboratory in Woods Hole, on Cape Cod, this species has been more thoroughly investigated in its developmental stages than any other echinoderm of North America. But a few years ago the supply suddenly dwindled and the scientists realized to their chagrin that they knew almost nothing about the ecological requirements of this favorite experimental animal. They knew that it ranged from rocky and shelly bottoms at moderate depth to the seaweeds in tide pools. There, presumably, each spring an adult urchin releases eggs (or sperm cells) into the sea to be fertilized by chance encounter and to start uncounted embryos on a course of growth among the drifting plankton. So far no one has been able to learn whether the disappearance of the purple urchins from so much of their former territory was due to excessive exploitation of adults, an unknown disease, currents that swept away the developing young, preventing them from settling close to their parents and renewing the population, or some other hazard (perhaps cold water) at this northern limit of their natural range.

Heart urchins are burrowers in muddy sand, and are rarely seen alive by beachcombers except soon after a storm that has washed the animal free and tossed it on the shore. On wet sand it can bury itself again, using its short spines and tube-feet to shift the particles from below its body and let itself sink to safety. A full grown *Clypeaster* or *Echinanthus* heart urchin, such as lives near the low-tide mark from coastal Carolinas southward, may be 6 inches long, almost 5 inches broad, and nearly 2 inches thick, yet bear spines less than 1/8 inch in length.

Sand dollars have a flattened body which seems to spread to a thin edge all around. Their spines are so short that a person must look closely to see that they are movable and active on a living specimen. Yet, with these spines, a sand dollar can sink itself quickly below the surface of a beach under water. It performs this disappearing act most obviously when it detects in the sea the flavor of a sea star (starfish) of any kind that feeds on sand dollars. Otherwise, when the tide is in, the sand dollars are likely to be moving slowly about on the sea floor, feeding on the organic detritus that settles there. Within their thin bodies they have a miniature jaw apparatus comparable to that of a sea urchin, and use it like a dredge for picking up particles of food.

From Long Island Sound northward and from the low-tide mark to a depth of 4,800 feet, the bottom-feeding fishes (such as cod, haddock and flounder) seek and eat the common circular sand dollar *(Echinarachnius parma)* of the Atlantic coast. Big ones are 3 inches in diameter and 3/8 inch thick at the center. Their symmetry is so regular on a radial plan that it is difficult to tell which part of the rim will be the advancing one when the animal moves along the bottom. The keyhole sand dollar *(Melitta quinquiesperforata)*, which is particularly numerous south of Cape Hatteras and into the West Indies and around the Gulf of Mexico, reveals its preference by developing notches around the rim at an early age. The first notch is between the petal-like patterns at the point in the rim that most usually trails behind. Four more notches form later, in line with each of the petal-like regions except the advancing one. With further growth, each long narrow notch is eventually closed, and remains as a slot through the body between upper and under surfaces. At Jeckyll Island, Georgia, we have seen dozens of these sand dollars either in the process of diving obliquely in slow motion into the sandy beach as the tide receded, or already hidden although recognizable because above them the sand maintained a slot or a depression matching these gaps in the shell of the self-buried animals. Deeper sandy bottoms of the Gulf of Mexico and of southern coasts in California are home to more elongate and bilaterally symmetrical sand dollars—the arrowheads *(Encope)* whose solid stony shells develop six notches or more and vary considerably in shape.

The Sea Stars (Class Asteroidea)

Of all the marine animals in the world, the type most widely recognized to be a denizen of saltwater only is the starfish, or more properly, the sea star. Nothing remotely resembling it lives in fresh waters or on land. Yet most people count the arms of the animal (and seem surprised if it has more than five) without realizing that these are merely lobes of the body and not appendages. Each arm contains a pair of outpocketings from the digestive tract and a pair of branches from the reproductive organs. In addition, a radial canal from the

Overleaf: left, Warty Sea Stars (Pisaster ochraceus); top right, Knobby Sea Star (Pisaster giganteus) eating a mussel (Mytilus); bottom, right, Knobby Sea Star (Pisaster giganteus capitatus)

water-vascular system extends the length of each arm and is connected to many dozens of pairs of extensile tube-feet that arise in a groove along the underside of the arm. The grooves all join at the mouth of the animal, which is ordinarily held close to whatever surface supports the sea star.

Beachcombers often learn to distinguish the three common orders of sea stars: the edged sea stars (Phanerozonia), the spiny sea stars (Spinulosa), and the forceps-carrying sea stars (Forcipulata). Each of these is well represented along the coasts of North America.

In an edged sea star, the upper surface of the body generally seems paved by close-fitting limy granules which extend to a rather definite boundary—often with a projecting fringe—separating it from the lower surface. Commonly, too, the tube-feet are pointed and lack the sucker tips that are customary in sea stars of other orders. This does not hamper the gliding movement of the mud star *(Ctenodiscus crispatus)*, which ranges from shallow water to 6,000 feet below the surface and from the Arctic southward along both coasts to South America. It grows to a length of 3 or 4 inches from tip to tip of its arms, and generally is a gray or ivory color that matches well the bottom on which it scavenges for food. Much more gaudy are the large purple or green or orange or yellow or brown reticulated sea stars *(Oreaster reticulatus)* of southern Florida and warm gulf coasts, and related species in southernmost California. These massive creatures often measure 16 inches in diameter, with pentagonal bodies two or more inches thick; the giants among them spread over a circle 20 inches across.

The spiny sea stars show no comparable demarcation between the upper and lower surfaces, and their bodies are roughened by a network of limy bars and overlapping plates that allow them flexibility while providing protection. The tube-feet usually have suction cups at the tips, allowing the sea star to cling tightly despite wave action. These animals include the sun stars, with eight or more arms, the sea bat *(Patiria miniata)* whose arms are joined by a thin webbing, the handsome little blood star *(Henricia sanguinolenta)*, and several different cushion stars with thicker bodies.

The sun star *Solaster endica,* found on North Atlantic coasts from Cape Cod to the Arctic and to the English Channel, and on North Pacific coasts as far south as Puget Sound, bears from nine to eleven arms spanning an area as much as 16 inches across. Seen often in shallow, sunlit water, it is generally reddish violet with a bright yellow plate like a medal to one side of center on the upper surface. A small relative, *S. caribbeus*, inhabits the coasts of Florida and the Gulf of Mexico, while one of intermediate size, *S. dawsoni*, lives on the Pacific coast. All are voracious feeders, eating smaller sea stars as well as snails, bivalves and sea anemones.

The sea bat, which may be 7 inches across, bright red or orange, is also a denizen of the Pacific. Found from Baja California to Alaska, it takes a mixed diet of seaweeds, sponges, squid eggs, snails and sea urchins. In an aquarium it will extend its thin stomach through its mouth to digest away the coating of diatoms that grows on the glass walls. The blood star is less than half this size, and comes in many hues. Its slender, pointed arms curve smoothly from the upper to the lower surface and bear an unusually narrow groove containing the delicate tube-feet. Commonly the blood star stands motionless atop a carpet of sponge, seeming to gain particles of food most easily where the encrusting colony is filtering the sea water. Blood stars are frequent on the Pacific coast from California to Alaska, and on the Atlantic side from Greenland to Cape Hatteras; they are among the few kinds of animals known from polar and temperate shallows as well as from great depths, and from the Arctic Ocean to the shores of Antarctica.

The cushion star *Pteraster miliaris* wears above its upper surface a strange weblike membrane. Below this the water circulates, entering from pores below and emerging through a large opening near the middle. The water-filled space serves both in respiration and as a brood chamber for the young cushion stars. These animals, like *Henricia* and *Solaster*, do not go through swimming larval stages, but remain under parental protection until they emerge from the relatively few, oversize, fertilized eggs as miniature stars.

Many of the forceps-carrying sea stars feed on bivalves, destroying oysters, clams and edible mussels at a rate that earns them the bitter enmity of shellfishermen. Until the men knew better, they broke in two and tossed back into the sea whatever sea stars of this type they found in the shellfish beds. Now they realize that both halves of the mutilated sea star can generally regenerate the missing parts, providing two sea stars where only one lived before. The forceps-carriers bear over their upper body surface large numbers of tiny pincers, called pedicellariae, each on a short flexible stalk; these special organs are used to keep the body clean. Generally the star itself has a relatively small central body area and long, rounded arms.

Members of the genus *Asterias* are the most widespread of the forceps-carriers. They are the common sea stars found clinging to wharf pilings and in tide pools over much of the world. The Pacific coast has *A. amurensis* from

Bipinnaria larva of a Sea Star

Alaska to Korea, the Atlantic coast *A. vulgaris* from Labrador to Long Island Sound (and more rarely southward), and *A. forbesi* from Maine to the Gulf of Mexico. Of these, *A. vulgaris* is the biggest, record specimens spanning an area 17 inches across. Often called the purple star, although it may be blue, or various shades of red, or variegated with yellow, purple or brown, it can be distinguished from *A. forbesi* (the "common sea star") by a pale yellow perforated plate on its back, rather than a bright orange-red one. The "common sea star" rarely grows to 11 inches across, but varies in color from purple through bronze, green and orange to brown.

All members of *Asterias* have four rows of strong, sucker-tipped tube-feet in the grooves below their arms, and use these in opening bivalves. Positioning itself opposite the hinge in a bivalve's shell, the sea star attaches firmly the tips of the tube-feet on two arms to one shell valve and those of the other three arms to the opposite shell valve. Then the sea star exerts its muscles, straining to open the bivalve while the mollusk inside strains to keep the shell valves

Brittle Star (Ophiopholis aculeata)

clamped together. Nor does the sea star need to wait until the bivalve tires. A force of 10 to 15 pounds per square inch, which the sea star can provide, suffices to bend the limy valves and open between them a slit 1/16 to 1/8 inch wide. Through this narrow gape the sea star can slide its filmy stomach. It everts the organ through its own mouth, into the shell cavity, and applies it to the body of the bivalve. While glands in the stomach wall secrete digestive juice, the sea star can relax, letting the shell valves pinch shut on the stalk portion of its stomach. But soon the digestive action kills the bivalve and the shell gapes readily. The sea star completes its meal, withdraws its stomach, and moves off.

Generally an *Asterias* has five arms. But some individuals have four, or six, or more rarely three or seven. The related polar sea star *(Leptasterias polaris)*, which has comparatively slender and less rough arms and inhabits cool coasts from Nova Scotia to Greenland, almost always has six arms; it may measure 12 inches across. But the giant among the forceps-carriers along American coasts is the sunflower star *(Pycnopodia helianthoides)* of California shorelines,

Overleaf: Basket Star (Gorgonocephalus arcticus)

where it continues to add more arms until it has as many as 20 and a spread of 30 inches or more. Except for the multitude of minute forceps on its body, it could easily be mistaken for a sun star. Its appetite seems proportional to its size, and it often swallows sea urchins whole.

The Serpent Stars (Class Ophiuroidea)

Of all echinoderms, the most active by far are the serpent stars or brittle stars from whose inflexible, disc-shaped body 5 (or rarely 6 or 7) slender arms extend, scarcely tapering between the distinct base and the outermost tip. A serpent star progresses rapidly over the bottom by snaky movements of its arms, below each of which are only tiny suckerless tube-feet that serve in capturing particles of food and passing them along toward the mouth below the center of the body. The name brittle star reflects the readiness of many of these animals to shed the end of any arm that is held, and regenerate it later. Generally the intact arms are five to six times as long as the diameter of the body, and in some serpent stars as much as fifteen times.

The beachcomber is most likely to meet serpent stars by turning over rocks in tide pools. The active animals will attempt to find another hiding place, but can often be scooped up for closer inspection. In a cupped hand they quickly react to the confinement and unfamiliar surface and slither out of the palmful of water to drop, perhaps back into the tide pool and safety. The circumtropical *Ophiactis savignyi* takes refuge while young in the cavities of large sponges, where it reproduces by transverse fission of the body. For a while, the new individuals regenerate 3 new arms on the new half of the body, and are hence 6-armed. But eventually, the self-mutilated animal produces only 2 new arms on the regenerated body and continues to adulthood with the characteristic five extensions that serve it in locomotion and feeding.

The daisy serpent star *(Ophiopholis aculeata)*, which is sometimes abundant in tide pools from Long Island Sound to the Arctic, varies so greatly in color of arms and body disc that it is almost impossible to find two alike. Professor Gairdner Moment of Goucher College has suggested that this may prevent a gull or other bird from recognizing any one pattern as a food item, in a reverse of mimicry serving as protective coloration. The body is often just under 1 inch across and red or blue, pink, yellow, brown, green or purple. The arms, to 3-1/2 inches long, generally contrast and are banded in deeper red or green or brown, perhaps alternating with white.

For no known reason, many of the serpent stars that live in deeper water are luminous at night. A few that possess this habit get caught in tide pools and can be discovered on a coastal field trip after dark. *Ophiacantha bidentata,* which is found along the west coast as far south as California and the east coast to the Carolinas, is most common below the 30-foot level; by day it is dark brown, and by night a bluish gray. Its arms often appear tangled into knots.

Serpent stars of a single species frequently cluster together in astonishing numbers, particularly on the bottom of tidal gutters. Apparently the tangle of interwining arms is more efficient as a trap for microscopic particles of food than any solitary serpent star could be while resting on the sediments. As though to exploit this rule, the members of one order of serpent stars have evolved whole forests of intertwining arms on each individual. Of these "basket stars," the best known is *Gorgonocephalus arcticus,* which has a body from 2-1/2 to 4 inches across and 5 arms that branch at the base, then fork repeatedly to a length of 14 inches. Small specimens can be found during minus tides between Nantucket Island and the Arctic. Larger ones in deeper water get caught on the dragging nets of fishermen and can be salvaged by the curious who visit fish piers while the fishing boats are being unloaded. If a specimen that is still alive is placed in fresh water, it will relax as it dies, spreading out and showing the maze of slender branchlets. It can then be preserved in a position that the animal might take on the sea floor, rather than curled up in a confusing mass. Actually, basket stars do cluster together or curl up separately where their arms are entwined around gorgonians and other anchored growths on the bottom. In groups or as clusters of their own making, they capture the minute food upon which they live and grow and reproduce. The name *Gorgonocephalus* is derived from the Greek words for Gorgon's head, a most appropriate designation recalling the mythical monster that had snakes instead of hair.

The Beard Worms *(Phylum Pogonophora)*

Well hidden from human view along the deeper portions of the continental slopes and in the abyssal trenches of the sea, beard worms remained totally unknown before 1914. By 1950 the number of kinds described in scientific journals had risen to three. Now it is well above 100. All of these creatures are extraordinarily slim—at least 100 times as long as broad—and live in delicate

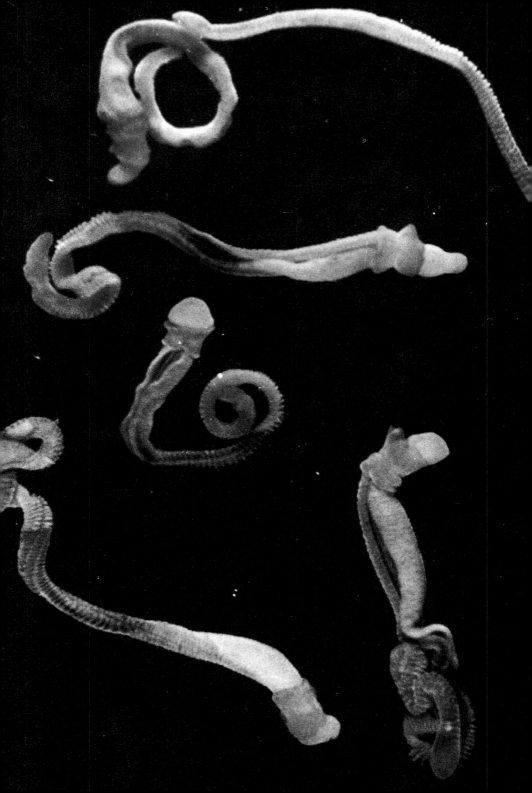

tubes of their own making. Uniquely among free-living animals with internal organs, they lack a digestive tract at all stages of development. Apparently they catch microscopic particles of food and digest it outside the body within the confines of a single spiral tentacle or a group of parallel tentacles arising from the most anterior part of the body. It is these fine tentacles that form the "beard" of the beard worm.

Along Arctic coasts, some beard worms live in much shallower water. They inhabit only greater depths along the Pacific coast of North America, and on the sea floor of the North Atlantic. After mating, female beard worms deposit their fertilized eggs beyond their tentacles in their tubular shelters, and apparently fast until the young have hatched and left to dig into the bottom and secrete tubes of their own. Similarities in embryonic development, particularly in formation of the body cavity, lead scientists to regard these strange animals as being related more closely to the acorn worms among the hemichords than to members of any other phylum.

The Acorn Worms and Their Kin
(Phylum Hemichordata)

Along many American coasts, a beachcomber can find an acorn worm by digging up a shovelful of muddy sand from the intertidal zone and washing it through a coarse fly screen. The trophy is usually a 5- to 6-inch worm that is too pale pink or ivory colored to be an earthworm, and too devoid of paired paddles or tentacles from the head to be a paddle-footed annelid of any kind. An acorn worm is unsegmented, but its body shows subdivision into an anterior proboscis, a short collar, and a long tapering trunk that could be compared to an anteater's tongue. The proboscis and collar on some species suggest an acorn in its cup. From these resemblances comes the name of the worldwide genus *Balanoglossus* ("acorn tongue"), and the popular name acorn worm (or tongue worm) for the animal.

The muscular proboscis serves in burrowing and in maintaining a U-shaped passageway in the sea floor, usually with a single back doorway where wastes are piled at intervals, and various branchings to several front doorways. Using cilia over the surface of its body, the worm glides backward and forward through its burrow. At the same time it maintains a current of water with oxygen

Sea Squirt (Ciona intestinalis)

and food particles into its mouth at the front of the collar below. The water plus carbon dioxide emerge from the ciliated pharynx through a long series of small gill slits that open through the trunk wall on each side for as much as a third of the body length. The pharyngeal slits and certain features of embryonic development so closely resemble the pattern seen in embryos of chordates that, until recently, the acorn worms and their kin were regarded as invertebrate chordates.

Balanoglossus is represented by an acorn worm *(B. aurantiacus)* along the Atlantic coast from Beaubort, N.C. to near Jacksonville, Florida, where it sometimes attains a length of 20 inches long in tidal mudflats. Its gill slits are narrow, as are those in members of the genus *Saccoglossus*, which have a long, pointed proboscis. Six-inch *S. kowalewskyi* ranges from North Carolina to Southern Maine; *3-inch S. pusillus*, which is brilliant orange, is sometimes abundant along southern California; still other species are found in the Gulf of Mexico. In shallows around the Florida Keys and at some places in the Gulf of Mexico, *Ptychodera bahamensis* represents a tropical genus whose members have a short, rounded proboscis and large conspicuous gill pores.

The acorn worms belong to Class Enteropneusta, all of which are marine, wormlike and solitary. The members of a second class (the Pterobranchia) are bottom dwellers in fairly deep water, diminutive or colonial, primarily distributed in the Southern Hemisphere, and so far unknown from American coasts.

The Invertebrate Chordates
(Phylum Chordata)

The ancestral chordates that led to almost 42,000 different kinds of chordates living in the modern world took the significant step of evolving a skull of some kind and blocklike vertebrae to form an axial skeleton. They are the widely-known vertebrates, about 50 of them in one small subphylum, Agnatha, with no jaws or paired appendages as lampreys and hagfishes, and the rest in the large subphylum, Gnathostomata, consisting of fishes, amphibians, reptiles, birds, and mammals. But two further ancestral lines led to existing animals with chordate features: a stiffening rod (notochord) of turgid cells, for which the phylum is named, just below a hollow dorsal nerve cord; paired gill slits through the pharyngeal walls; and a postanal tail at some stage in development. One of the two has been hailed as the nearest survivor to the ancestral chordate, despite peculiar characteristics such as a notochord and nerve cord extending from end to end of the body and a strange inpocketing of the ventral body wall to form a special chamber (the atrium) into which the gill slits open and discharge water toward the outside world; these are the lancelets or "amphioxi" (meaning pointed at both ends) of 25 species in 2 genera in the order Leptocardii of subphylum Cephalochordata. The other chordates that produce no cranium have no body cavity or segmental pattern either; they are the tunicates of about 1,300 kinds in three orders of the subphylum Tunicata (or Urochordata). Tunicates and lancelets are all marine.

The Lancelets (Subphylum Cephalochordata)

Where a clear sandy beach is exposed by a minus tide between Chesapeake Bay and the West Indies, and in the superficial sediments of similar beaches in

Sea Pork colonies (Amaroucium constellatum)
232

southern California and southward, slim little flattened pinkish creatures embed themselves tail downward and suck in a current of water through an oval mouth opening fringed with sensitive tentacles. Those of the East Coast mature to a length of about 2 inches; the West Coast species *(Branchiostoma californiense)* at 4 inches is the largest of the group. Two of the Atlantic species of lancelets belong to this genus, and the other two to *Asymmetron* because they develop gonads along only one side. This continues a mild asymmetry characteristic of all lancelet larvae, which drift among the plankton in a vertical (mouth-up) position before becoming filter-feeders in the sand. Lancelets are widespread in this habitat throughout the temperate and tropical world. Fishes are their principal predators.

The Tunicates (Subphylum Tunicata or Urochordata)

In his *History of Animals,* Aristotle described what he could discover inside an ascidian pulled from its area of permanent attachment to a rock along the coast. Many a beachcomber, exploring a tide pool in American waters, has found these animals and been equally puzzled by them. As sessile and maturing individuals, they secrete about themselves a unique tunic (hence "tunicate") that often includes cellulose. It has two openings, one a mouth and the other a combined discharge site for water that has been filtered of food particles and oxygen while passing through gill slits in the capacious pharynx, and for wastes. Almost no other organs can be seen inside the U-shaped body. Yet, when jarred or nudged, the animal reacts by contracting vigorously, expelling water through both openings and earning its alternative name of sea squirt.

Tunicate larvae are free-swimming, less than 1/4-inch long, and tadpole-like in having an egg-shaped body and short, slender, propulsive tail; the tail contains the notochord. After a brief pelagic life among the plankton, an ascidian larva cements itself to a support, loses its tail and notochord, in a degenerative transformation that obliterates most signs of chordate connections. The body may be 2-1/2 to 3 inches long and pinkish orange in the plump sea peach *(Tethyum pyriformis,* formerly *Halocynthia)* of the Atlantic coast from Maine northward; or so slender and translucent yellowish green as to suggest a 3-inch length of small intestine, like *Ciona intestinalis* on wharf pilings along the shores of California and of New England and the eastern provinces of Canada. It may consist of separate globular individuals, like the "green beads" *(Perophora viridis)* that arise from a slender connecting stolon; or a firm, compact colony

Overleaf: left, Stalked Tunicate (Styela montereyensis); right, Pelagic Tunicate (Salpa sp.)

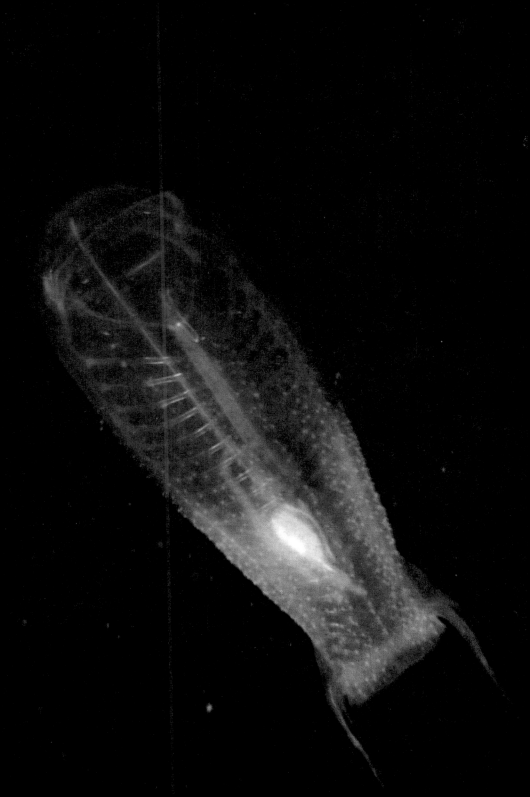

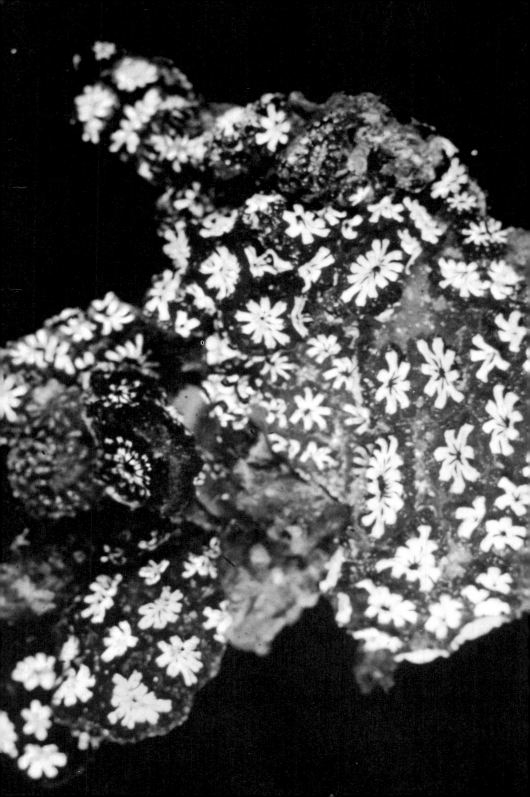

such as "sea pork" *(Amaroucium)* 4/5 inch thick and 4 to 8 inches in other dimensions, in which the many individuals are interconnected but in inconspicuous starlike clusters.

Occasionally, in tide pools or coastal waters or among flotsam along the beach, other tunicates turn up, representing the two classes or permanently pelagic species. The visitor may be a larvacean (class Larvacea), such as an *Appendicularia*, that never outgrows its larval body form although it becomes sexually mature and secretes about its diminutive self a gelatinous tunic that is abandoned and replaced whenever it ceases to assist the tunicate in gathering microscopic food. Or the tunicate may be a thaliacean (class Thaliacea), such as a salp *(Salpa)* whose delicate, transparent, barrel-shaped body is propelled by contraction of separate, whitish, encircling bands of muscle; or such as a colonial pyrosome (*Pyrosoma*—the "fire body") 3 inches long and 3/4 inch in diameter, forming a cylinder composed of many minute individuals that discharge their waste water into a central cavity and then to the outside world, driving themselves along. At night, if stimulated in any way, a pyrosome luminesces brilliantly and then fades away. While observing these amazing animals in their natural habitat, it is indeed hard to think of them as offshoots from the same chordate ancestry that led to fish and man.

Colonial Tunicate (Botryllus schlosseri)

Bibliography

Abbott, R. Tucker, *Seashells of North America* (New York: Golden Press; 1968)

Buchsbaum, Ralph, and Lorus J. Milne, with Mildred Buchsbaum and Margery Milne, *The Lower Animals: Living Invertebrates of the World* (Garden City, N.Y.: Doubleday; 1960)

Galtsoff, Paul S. (coordinator), *Gulf of Mexico: Its Origin, Waters, and Marine Life* (Washington, D.C.: U.S. Fish and Wildlife Service, 1954) as Bull. 89. Protozoa (Victor Sprague); Porifera (J. Q. Tierney; F. G. W. Smith); Coelenterata (E. S. Deevey, Jr.; Mary Sears; J. W. Hedgpeth; F. W. Bayer; F. G. Walton Smith); Ctenophora (Mary Sears); Platyhelminthes (L. H. Hyman; H. W. Manter; A. C. Chandler); Nemertea (W. R. Coe); Echinoderida (B. G. Chitwood); Nematoda (B. G. Chitwood and R. W. Timm; Asa C. Chandler); Chaetognatha (E. L. Pierce); Acanthocephala (A. C. Chandler); Bryozoa (R. C. Osburn); Brachiopoda (G. A. Cooper); Phoronida (J. W. Hedgpeth); Enteropneusta (J. W. Hedgpeth); Echinodermata (A. H. Clark; Elisabeth Deichmann); Tardigrada (B. G. Chitwood); Annelida (Olga Hartman); Echiurida, Sipunculida (J. W. Hedgpeth); Xiphosura, Pycnogonida (J. W. Hedgpeth); Ostracoda (W. L. Tressler); Copepoda (W. L. Schmitt); Cirripedia (Dora P. Henry); Mysidacea and Euphausiacea (A. H. Banner); Stomatopoda (F. A. Chace, Jr.); Decapoda (Elinor H. Behre); Mollusca (F. G. W. Smith; Harald A. Rehder; Gilbert L. Voss); Tunicata (W. G. Van Name); Cephalochordata (J. W. Hedgpeth)

Levi, Herbert W., and Lorna R. Levi, *Spiders and Their Kin* (New York: Golden Press; 1968)

Miner, Roy W., *Field Book of Seashore Life* (New York: G. P. Putnam's Sons; 1950)

Pennak, Robert W., *Fresh-water Invertebrates of the United States* (New York: Ronald Press; 1953)

Pratt, Henry S., *A Manual of the Common Invertebrate Animals* (New York: McGraw-Hill; 1935)

Ricketts, Edward F., and Jack Calvin, *Between Pacific Tides* (Stanford, Calif.: Stanford University Press; rev. Joel W. Hedgpeth, 1952)

Smith, Ralph I. (ed.), *Keys to Marine Invertebrates of the Woods Hole Region* (Woods Hole: Marine Biological Laboratory; 1964)

Ward, Henry B., and George C. Whipple, *Fresh-water Biology* (New York: John Wiley & Sons; rev. W. T. Edmondson, 1959)

Zim, Herbert S., and Lester Ingle, *Seashores* (New York: Golden Press, 1955)

Index

242

243

245

CREDITS

(credits read from top to bottom and from left to right)
Half-title page, Hugh Spencer; Title page, Ron Church; page 12 (both), Ron Church; 13, Fred Roberts, Ron Church, J. A. L. Cooke; 16, Hugh Spencer; 19, Western Marine Laboratory; 21, Ralph Buchsbaum; 23, Western Marine Laboratory; 25, General Biological Supply House; 28, Western Marine Laboratory; 30, Ron Church; 31, William Amos, Jeff Meyer from Photofind (both); 34, Lorus and Margery Milne; 37, Hugh Spencer; 38, Ron Church; 42, John Boland from Photofind, Ron Church; 43, Ralph Buchsbaum; 45, Jack Dermid; 46, John Boland from Photofind; 47 (both), John Boland from Photofind; 50, Ron Church; 51, Robert Ames from Photofind; 52, Ron Church; 53, Ralph Buchsbaum; 54, Ron Church; 56, Don Wobber from Photofind; 58 (both), John Boland from Photofind; 59, John Boland from Photofind, Ron Church; 63, J. A. L. Cooke; 66, J. A. L. Cooke; 67, Edward S. Ross; 70, Western Marine Laboratory; 71, Western Marine Laboratory; 73, Lorus and Margery Milne; 76, Ralph Buchsbaum; 77, Western Marine Laboratory; 79, J. A. L. Cooke; 80, Lorus and Margery Milne; 90, William Amos, Systematics-Ecology Program at Marine Biological Laboratory Woods Hole; 94, William Amos; 95, William Amos; 98, Ralph Buchsbaum; 102, Don Wobber from Photofind; 103, Ralph Buchsbaum; 105, Western Marine Laboratory; 106, Western Marine Laboratory; 107, Don Wobber from Photofind; 109, Ralph Buchsbaum, Lorus and Margery Milne; 110, Robert Ames from Photofind, Ron Church; 111, Ralph Buchsbaum; 113, Ralph Buchsbaum; 115, Lynwood Chace; 116, Ralph Buchsbaum; 119, Edward S. Ross; 120, Lynwood Chace; 121, Lynwood Chace; 122, Ron Church; 123, Ron Church, Dan Gotshall, Robert Ames from Photofind; 126, Ron Church, Ralph Buchsbaum; 127, Jeff Meyer from Photofind; 128, Woodbridge Williams; 129, Ralph Buchsbaum; 131, Ralph Buchsbaum; 135, Ron Church; 136, Fritz Goro; 139 (both), Ralph Buchsbaum; 141, William Tucker; 144, Ralph Buchsbaum; 146, J. A. L. Cooke, Ron Church; 150, Jeff Meyer from Photofind; 152, Ralph Buchsbaum; 158 (both), J. A. L. Cooke; 159 (both), J. A. L. Cooke; 161, Woodbridge Williams; 162 (both), J. A. L. Cooke; 163, William Amos from Systematics-Ecology Program at Marine Biological Laboratory Woods Hole; 165, Edward S. Ross; 166, Western Marine Laboratory; 170, Jeff Meyer from Photofind; 172, Edward S. Ross, J. A. L. Cooke; 174, Ron Church; Fred Roberts; 177, Lynwood Chace, David C. Stager; 178, Dan Gotshall; 180, Woodbridge Williams; 181, Jack Dermid; 182 (both), Edward S. Ross; 183, Ralph Buchsbaum; 184, Edward S. Ross; 187, Edward S. Ross, J. A. L. Cooke; 189, Fritz Goro; 190 (both), Edward S. Ross; 191, Edward S. Ross; 193, Edward S. Ross; 194, Fred Roberts; 195, J. A. L. Cooke, Edward S. Ross; 196, J. A. L. Cooke; 197, Edward S. Ross; 198, Edward S. Ross; 199, Edward S. Ross, J. A. L. Cooke, Edward S. Ross; 201, Edward S. Ross; 202, Edward S. Ross; 203, William Amos; 205, William Amos; 208, John Boland from Photofind; 210, Ron Church; 211, Dan Gotshall, Don Wobber from Photofind; 213, Ron Church, Lorus and Margery Milne; 214, Ron Church; 215, Jeff Meyer from Photofind, Ralph Buchsbaum; 218, Ralph Buchsbaum; 219, Western Marine Laboratory, John Boland from Photofind; 222, J. A. L. Cooke; 223, Systematics-Ecology Program at Marine Biological Laboratory Woods Hole; 224, Lorus and Margery Milne; 228, Ralph Buchsbaum; 230, J. A. L. Cooke; 232, Systematics-Ecology Program at Marine Biological Laboratory Woods Hole; 234, Ron Church; 235, Dan Gotshall; 236, Systematics-Ecology Program at Marine Biological Laboratory Woods Hole. Map and diagram by Elaine Jones.

The Animal Life of North America series (six volumes) is prepared and produced
by Chanticleer Press:
Publisher: Paul Steiner
Editor: Milton Rugoff. *Associates:* Susan Weiley, Joanne Shapiro, Jean Walker
Art Director: Ulrich Ruchti, assisted by Elaine Jones
Production: Gudrun Buettner, assisted by Helga Lose
Printed by Amilcare Pizzi, S.p.A., Milan, Italy